THE
MAGNIFICENT
ONE

The Story of Mario Lemieux

Michael McKinley

Grosset & Dunlap

ISBN: 0-448-42554-8   A B C D E F G H I J

Designer: fiwired.com

Published by Grosset & Dunlap, a division of Penguin Putnam Books for Young Readers, 345 Hudson Street, New York, NY 10014. GROSSET & DUNLAP is a trademark of Penguin Putnam Inc. Published simultaneously in Canada.

Printed in Hong Kong

Cover photo credits:
Large photo: Jim McIsaac/Bruce Bennett Studios
Inset photo, right: Jim McIsaac/Bruce Bennett Studios
Inset photo, left: Dave Sandford/Hockey Hall of Fame

CONTENTS

Prologue

The autumn leaves had just begun to fall on the NHL's 84th season, and with them dropped a rumor. This was not the kind of rumor the hockey world expects, like one about players being traded. Or about a coach being fired. Or about a promising rookie being called up from the minors. Those who didn't believe in magic shrugged it off as just more mischief on the part of a restless media early in the season.

But the people who believed in magic dared to believe the rumor might be true. If it was, older fans could once again marvel at one of the NHL's truly inspired talents while younger fans who know only the legend could finally witness for themselves the magic that is Mario Lemieux.

When Mario left hockey in 1997, it looked like he was gone for good. He had been suffering from terrible back pain, and worse, complaining that the game was no longer fun. And yet, in early November 2000, as the autumn chill settled in, Mario Lemieux was once again out on the ice, skating in his long, graceful stride, getting himself ready to play. Hockey fans rejoiced because now they knew that the rumor was indeed true: Mario Lemieux, the greatest Pittsburgh Penguin ever (some would say the greatest hockey player ever), was coming out of retirement. He was coming back to light up the NHL again.

From 1984 to 1997, when he made the yellow and black of Pittsburgh jersey with a number 66 on the back famous around the world, Mario Lemieux won almost everything the NHL had to offer. He had been injured and missed entire seasons. He had battled back from severe illness, and lived to tell about it. And now, he was going to risk everything to give it one more shot.

When Mario Lemieux first announced that he was planning to lace up his skates one more time, another rumor began to surface. This one was a dark whisper that he was coming back to the NHL because of money. Mario Lemieux had also done something that no NHL player had ever done after he retired: he bought the team that he had made famous. Now, though, his team was showing signs of fading, and so, by putting on his skates again as a Penguin, some said Mario Lemieux was simply protecting his investment. By coming back to play, he would help the Penguins to make more money, and thus earn more money for himself. Why else would he bother? He had already won every award and broken records, and besides, he had said when he retired that the game of hockey as he knew it, with clutching and grabbing and slashing and tackling, was something that no longer interested him. What had changed?

Mario Lemieux was quick to take on his critics with a disarmingly simple answer: "It *is* good for business," he admitted, "but it is my passion for hockey that brought me back." After three and a half years of watching hockey from the stands, Mario Lemieux missed the game. He missed being out there in his kingdom of ice, his hockey stick a kind of sorcerer's wand with which he could do impossible things with the puck. He missed the friendship of his teammates, the easy banter of the locker room. He missed the junior hockey kind of fun of winter road trips, when you could kid around with the boys, even if the road trips in the NHL were made in private jets, and not in drafty buses. He missed the roar of the crowd when he and his teammates would do something so beautiful with the puck that it surprised even them. But most of all, he was sorry that four-year-old Austin, his youngest child, had never seen him play. Sure, he and Austin had watched old videos of Dad playing hockey, but it wasn't the same. He wanted to show his boy what the old man could do.

So, two days after Christmas, Austin Lemieux stood in awe as the huge banner bearing his father's famous number 66 was lowered from the rafters of Pittsburgh's Mellon Arena. The number that had been retired when its owner hung up his skates was now back in action. Amidst the excitement was the question nagging at the hearts of even the most loyal fans. Could Mario Lemieux dazzle us once more?

CHAPTER ONE

The Gift

The neighbors had to blink twice to make sure they weren't dreaming. There, in front of the modest red brick duplex at 6700 rue Jogues, in the working-class West End of Montreal, Pierrette Lemieux was shoveling snow. Not that there was anything unusual about shoveling snow in winter in Montreal, where the snow can pile up so high that it's hard to open your front door. What was unusual in this winter of 1968, was that Madame Lemieux was shoveling snow from her front walk and *bringing it inside her house.*

The neighbors didn't know what to think. They liked the Lemieuxs, who seemed a normal family. There was Pierrette, who stayed at home to look after her kids, and her husband Jean-Guy, a construction worker, and three boys, Alain, Richard, and the youngest, Mario. The neighbors thought that maybe the Lemieuxs had run out of hot water, and were melting snow on their stove, so they could bathe. Madame Lemieux's sisters, however, were more blunt, their French straining with disbelief as they asked: "*T'es folle, Pierrette?*" ("Are you crazy?")

Pierrette Lemieux, her cheeks flushed with effort, would shoot back with absolute certainty that no, she was not crazy. She was looking toward the future.

"Besides," she would say, "the carpets are of good quality. They can take it."

The carpets? Pierrette Lemieux was bringing snow inside her house to put it on the carpet? What would she be doing in summer? Running the lawnmower over the carpets?

Pierrette Lemieux was not thinking about summer. She wasn't even thinking all that much about winter. She was thinking of her youngest son Mario. Even though he was only three years old, Mario had to go through the same ritual that her older boys had gone through. Madame Lemieux needed to build an ice rink on her carpet, so that little Mario could learn to skate, so that he could play hockey.

Each afternoon in that winter of 1968, Mario Lemieux, future NHL superstar, would take his first halting steps in skates on the snow-packed carpet, safe from the elements and the bigger, faster skaters, who might accidentally run him over. Under the watchful eye of his mother, young Mario learned to push and glide. Just to make sure that the "ice" stayed hard, Madame Lemieux used nature as an air conditioner, turning off the heat and keeping the front door of 6700 rue Jogues open. The cold air would whip in off the street, and Mario would skate on the carpet.

People passing by, their heads hunched against the blowing snow, would glance at the house with the open front door and they would shake their heads: those Lemieuxs certainly were different. Only two years later, people would begin to get an idea of just how different they really were.

Late on a weekday afternoon in the winter of 1970, Pierrette and Jean-Guy escorted young Mario five blocks down the road to an ice rink behind St. Jean de Mantha church, where the family would worship on Sundays. School had just let out for the day and excited school kids were already out on the ice, impressing their parents as they sprayed ice chips into the air, imitating their heroes on the Montreal Canadiens. Jean-Guy Lemieux took Mario into the shack next to the rink and helped him tie his skates. After all, the boy had just turned five a couple of months earlier.

Mario had been taking skating lessons at the Arena Municipal Georges et Sylvio Mantha, tucked amid the concrete pillars of the freeway that leads from Montreal to Ottawa. The arena had been named after the Mantha brothers who had been stars for the Montreal Canadiens in the 1920s and '30s. Every kid who played in the arena dreamed of one day wearing the famous *bleu, blanc, et rouge* (blue, white, and red) jersey of the Canadiens. To Fernand Fichaud, Mario's skating coach, it looked as if the Lemieuxs' youngest son had the best chance of any kid he had seen.

Fichaud had taught Mario how to skate by having him push a little chair in front of him until he learned to stand on his own. As soon as he could, Fichaud gave Mario a hockey stick and puck. He believed that if young players learned how to handle a stick and a puck while they were learning how to skate, they would instinctively feel that the actions naturally belonged together.

In the autumn of 1969, Mario was just four years old. He hadn't even mastered the art of talking, but he did something on the ice that startled his coach. Mario picked up the puck at center ice and skated around several kids his own age. Once in the clear, he had a breakaway on the equally young goalie. Now, a breakaway at age four is a lot different than at age 14, or 24. Everything is much, much slower, with the skater lurching in trying to keep the puck on the stick. Not so for Mario.

As Fichaud looked on, Mario closed in on the goalie and pulled the puck hard to his right. The goalie moved with him. As soon as the goalie moved, Mario, still skating, pulled the puck back to his left. With the goalie now out of position, Mario shot it into the empty net.

Fichaud was amazed; he hadn't taught Mario how to deke. He hadn't ever seen a child that young do anything of the sort, not even Lemieux's older brothers, Alain and Richard, who were clearly talented hockey players. The coach knew that this kid was going to be great.

Mario's parents also knew they had something special. They were looking forward to showing him off on the outdoor rink, though they were still uncertain how he would behave. Maybe he would be overwhelmed by the noise and motion and the older, faster skaters. Maybe he would start to cry and want to go home.

Little Mario came out of the shack, his hockey stick in one hand, a puck in the other. He looked at the bigger kids zipping around the ice as if they were Yvan Cournoyer, or Jean Beliveau, or Henri Richard, all Stanley Cup Champions with Montreal. Then Mario stepped out onto the ice, and suddenly everyone was looking at him. This little five-year-old took off through the crowd as if he was on an overtime breakaway in Game 7 of the Stanley Cup Finals.

All the parents stopped talking and just watched Mario, some of them exclaiming, "Look at this little guy, look at him skate!" All those days spent skating on the family carpet in the front room of the red brick house and pushing a chair on the ice of the Mantha Arena seemed to have paid off far greater than anyone could have imagined. Even so, Pierrette Lemieux knew that her son's amazing ability wasn't the result of any childish steps on her carpet. It certainly wasn't anything that had been passed on to him by his moderately athletic parents. "That," she said about her young son's startling hockey ability, "that came from the sky. It's a natural gift. No one in the family gave it to him." And in the coming years, people would see just how great was that gift.

CHAPTER TWO

The Best

In French, Mario Lemieux's surname means "the best." Just a year after that day on the outdoor rink behind the church of St. Jean de Mantha, when Mario made the adults gasp in awe, people were seeing that young Mario was living up to his name.

In 1971, Mario was six years old, playing hockey at the "mosquito" level. He went to watch his ten-year-old brother Alain's peewee game. It was just an exhibition match, but Mario was excited to watch the older boys play. Alain's coach was equally excited to have Mario there. So much so that he went into the stands and asked Mario to join the game. Mario took one look at the boys on the ice who were three or four years older than he was — and he said yes.

Playing with the big kids, Mario scored a goal and an assist. If people hadn't heard about him before, they would now.

By the time Mario was eight years old, he was the star of the Ville Emard Hurricanes. At tournaments around the province of Quebec, news that Mario was playing would drive attendance from the hundreds into the thousands. People wanted to see this hockey genius who could score five or six goals a game, and who even had a *slapshot*. One with power, and distance, and accuracy. And he was just a kid!

There were people who did not want to see Mario's talent, and especially not his slapshot, and they were the kids playing goal against him. One young goalie who played for St. Joseph's, worried himself to sleep before his game against Mario. He knew what was coming, and it wasn't going to be pretty.

Sure enough, not long after the opening face-off, the goalie saw his worst nightmare coming true. Mario was skating in on him alone. The St. Joseph's goalie prepared to follow the puck — he knew how fancy young Mario could be with his dekes. Mario Lemieux, however, wasn't going to deke anyone; he was going to blast a hole through the goalie. He raised his stick and let rip with a slapshot, one so hard and fast that the young goaltender didn't even have time to move out of the way. The puck could have hit him in his shoulder pads, or his leg pads, or even on his mask, but as bad luck would have it, Mario's slapshot nailed the goalie in his unprotected neck. He crumpled to the ice in tears. His teammates tried to make him feel better — "at least Mario didn't score" — but he wasn't buying. The game was far from over. Mario would be back.

The goalie's prediction came true shortly afterward, when to his horror, he saw Mario Lemieux skating in on him alone again. Worse, much, much worse, Mario had his stick raised for another killer slapshot. Thinking quickly, the terrified goalie decided to take the least painful option. He skated hard to the corner of the rink, as far from danger as he could get. Mario, a touch surprised, lowered his stick, skated in on goal, and popped the puck in the empty net. He looked over at the relieved goalie and smiled the kind of smile that said, "I win."

As a young blossoming star, Mario loved to win, but most of all, he loved to win against his older brothers. On those days when it was too stormy to spend their usual five or six hours skating on the outdoor rink behind St. Jean de Mantha church, the Lemieux brothers could be found playing hockey in their basement. Having grown up learning to skate on their living-room floor, they weren't about to show any respect to the basement when it came to hockey.

Sometimes they used big spoons, sometimes shortened sticks; sometimes they used bottle tops, sometimes plastic pucks. With whatever they could get their hands on, the Lemieux brothers would recreate "Hockey Night in Canada" in their basement. They smashed the tile floor, chipped the piano keys, and bashed the ceiling with deflected shots. Mario competed fiercely against his brothers. When he beat them, the world was as it should be. When he did not, his father Jean-Guy said, "It would be as if a hurricane went through the basement."

Not everyone was impressed by Mario's drive to win, and soon it created problems for him, ones that would last for years. Wayne Gretzky, who was five years ahead of Mario, and already famous in Canada, was still a skinny teenager. Mario was bigger than the other kids. While

Gretzky received his fair share of hits, there was a sense that you didn't hit him — even if you could — because he might break. Mario, standing taller than everyone else in his number 27 jersey, looked like he could take a hit. And that he needed one.

Mario Lemieux has taken many hits from the press and from hockey fans during his pro career, and many of them have come off the ice. People have said nasty things about him because of what they call his arrogance — that mixture of pride and superiority. The thinking is that anyone who has a great talent should be humble about it and not try to show up other people. What they didn't understand was that while Mario was talented, he was angry, too.

He didn't enjoy having the wives of opposing coaches and mothers of opposing players spit on him because he was good. He didn't enjoy having to have his teammates escort him like bodyguards when he went to the snack bar of a visiting rink, for fear opposing players and their parents would attack him. Most of all, he didn't enjoy having opposing players run at him with their sticks, and slash his body with such force that he looked like he'd been beaten up by a gang. Once, when his fame was beginning to grow, a photographer from the *Ottawa Citizen* wanted to take Mario's picture, but his coach said no. Mario was so bruised from the game that it looked as if he was suffering from child abuse.

Mario, though, was no angel, and even from a young age, he used to get even with players who took cheap shots at him. Both his teammates and opponents would remark that he wasn't shy about using his hockey stick as a weapon. In fact, he was very skilled at slashing players on the lower calf if they tried to get physical with him. His coaches would tell Lemieux to stay calm and to take the hits. But he wouldn't always listen, and he often wound up in the penalty box.

Mario's favorite method of revenge was on the score sheet. Opposing players soon learned that making him angry could have serious consequences. In one game, Lemieux took so many bad penalties against a team from Verdun that his coach benched him. Imagine making a player who would become one of the NHL's greatest scorers ever ride the pine. Mario was shocked, and he broke down in tears. It didn't matter. His team was losing 6-1. He had hurt them with his undisciplined play.

In the final period, his coach put him out on the ice. Though the game was lost, Mario had promised to play smart, disciplined hockey. He knew what kind of tongue-lashing he would get from his father after the game, and he hoped to at least get a goal in his own defense. The fans had booed him, and he was embarrassed. He wanted to show everyone that he could do better.

That night, the team from Verdun discovered that you didn't ever want to embarrass Mario Lemieux. In the final 20 minutes of the game, Lemieux scored six goals — a double hat trick — to lead his team to a 7-6 win. Everyone who witnessed his performance was aston-ished, especially the opposing players, who crumbled under his one-man attack. And if there were any doubters in the stands that night, they were now inclined to believe that what people said was true. This kid from the Ville Emard was going to be the best.

CHAPTER THREE

The Next Quebec Savior

It has been said that in Quebec, hockey is a religion, and the Montreal Canadiens are its high priests. The Canadiens won their unequaled 24 Stanley Cups in one of hockey's greatest shrines, a place called The Forum. Though the Canadiens are struggling today and have moved from The Forum to the Molson Centre, The Forum was the temple of hockey when Mario Lemieux was a boy and it was only a ten-minute walk from his house. Inside this temple, the men who wore the fabled red, white, and blue jerseys would make magic on ice as regularly as snow fell on Montreal in winter.

When Mario was a teenager, all of Montreal was in love with the man known as "The Flower," which is the English translation of the surname of Guy Lafleur. "The Flower" had been picked number one overall by Montreal in the 1971 NHL Amateur Draft. And before that he had been the star of the Quebec Major Junior Hockey League (QMJHL). In fact, he had been more than a star — he had been a superhero, shattering all records on his way to scoring 130 goals and 79 assists in his final junior season as he led his team, the Quebec Remparts, to win the championship Memorial Cup.

Mario Lemieux and his bantam teammates knew that while Lafleur had been heaped with talent by the hockey gods, he also worked hard. Everyone knew that Lafleur couldn't shoot backhand when he was a kid, so he practiced for hours alone, with a bucket of pucks. They knew how "The Flower" used to go to the rink before school and just practice skating. And they knew the kind of records he set in junior hockey.

Mario Lemieux also knew what people were saying about him: he could be the next one. Yes, the boy from Ville Emard could be the next great player to come out of Quebec and keep the province's reputation as a superstar factory alive. He was off to a good start.

When Mario was 11 years old, he was named Player of the Month in his Montreal minor hockey group. The Canadiens had a night where they would honor all such star players from around the city by inviting them to The Forum to have their pictures taken with the Montreal Canadien who had been Player of the Month for the NHL team. Mario Lemieux got to pose for his first photo with his hero, Guy Lafleur. Mario knew what was expected of him, and he would sometimes think, "If only I could be as good as Lafleur..."

But first he had to get through bantam hockey, wearing the black uniform of the Ville Emard Hurricanes, whose jerseys featured a kamikaze pelican with a big scar on its face. The image was fun but also said, "Don't mess with us." The bantam Lemieux was coached by Ron Stevenson, a tough Montreal detective who wouldn't let his players get away with any kind of spoiled behavior. There was no swearing. Players wore jackets and ties on road trips. They had curfews, which, if broken, resulted in even stricter curfews. And Stevenson practiced his teams hard, five out of seven days a week, in addition to the three games a week that they played. If any player made a bad play out on the ice, Stevenson would have him write 100 lines — as if in school — "I will not make bad plays. I will not make bad plays…" No one was excused from the system — not even Mario Lemieux, who had to write 100 lines for taking bad penalties or for not back-checking.

Stevenson's practices were hard and intense, and so was the style of hockey that the Hurricanes played. Led by Mario at center, future NHLers J.J. Daigneault and Marc Bergevin on defense, and wingers Sylvain Cote and Stephane Lepage, the Hurricanes won the provincial championship three out of the four years that Mario played and Stevenson coached him.

Stevenson recalled that Mario and his linemates would practice as hard as they played, sometimes skating for hours without the puck. In one practice, Mario Lemieux skated in on the defense, then made a brilliant pass to linemate Lepage, who was racing down the ice behind him. Brilliant because it was smack on the tape of Lepage's stick, and Mario hadn't even turned his head to look. When Coach Stevenson asked him how he knew it was Lepage behind him, Mario replied, "I could tell by the sound of his skates."

Though Mario worked hard on the ice, it seemed to some as if he was spoiled and lazy off the ice. And the person who got the blame for it was his mother. Though Mario was learning to be careful when around strangers, he was lively and open at home, especially with his mother Pierrette.

The two were very close but some felt Pierrette allowed Mario too much freedom. Mario was allowed to stay up as late as he wanted and to sleep in all day — even if it meant missing school. And, like most teenagers, Mario loved to sleep! He could sleep for 14 hours at a stretch.

Though Mario was a good student, school was not as important to his mother or to him as was his success in hockey. And he was playing hockey a lot: regular season games, playoffs and tournaments, practices, plus games with his friends on the local rink. Mario was playing hockey two or three times a day throughout the winter. School would be sacrificed so that Mario could get some rest and be ready for the next game.

Though he might miss school, Mario was never too tired or too ill to play hockey. Once, his mother called Coach Stevenson to say that Mario had the flu, and that he would not be able to play that afternoon. Mario had never missed a game or a practice, so the coach was surprised. However, shortly before the Hurricanes were going to take to the ice, Mrs. Lemieux showed up with her boy. She had to bring him, she told the coach, or Mario would have destroyed the house. In his four years under Coach Stevenson, Mario never missed a game or a practice, even if he did miss a good deal of school.

By the time Mario was 12 years old, the Montreal Canadiens were already checking him out. The Canadiens great winger Yvan "The Roadrunner" Cournoyer, a player who was so fast it seemed as if someone had set his skates on fire, went to watch Mario's bantam team play in a tournament. He returned to Montreal and told his coach, Scotty Bowman, that he had to check out this kid who played for Ville Emard. Bowman, one of the NHLs brightest coaching stars, was not easily impressed. He skeptically went to see Lemieux play, then came back to Montreal and spoke to a city newspaper reporter. "We're running all over the world looking for talent, and last week, in our own backyard, I saw the best prospect that I've ever seen."

The best prospect that Bowman, who would win eight Stanley Cups and more games than any other coach in NHL history, had ever seen. It was a staggering compliment. If Mario Lemieux had read the newspaper, he would have been thrilled. And he probably would have been a bit scared, too. Imagine the pressure of being told when you were only a kid that you had such a great future ahead of you. On the one hand, you'd be happy about what was to come, but on the other hand you would also be asking yourself, "What happens if I fail?"

Now that Mario was 14, and in his last year of bantam hockey, he was attracting the attention of critics who were asking the same question. Sure, he had gobs of natural talent, so much so that he could cruise around the ice as if out for a Sunday skate with his granny, and he would still

23

put up fabulous points. But his point total was nowhere near as good as that English kid, Wayne Gretzky, who was at that time on his way to NHL stardom, having already won his first Hart Trophy as the league MVP. Everyone had raved about Gretzky when he was a kid, and everyone was raving about him now that he was a pro. Even when he was just a peewee, Gretzky had the desire to be the best — you could see it in everything he did.

Mario knew that if all went well, he would be playing junior hockey in another year, and as soon as he laced on his skates for his first junior team, the comparisons to Lafleur — and to Gretzky — would become official. Mario badly wanted to win his last game as a bantam player, and send a message to the world that he could be as good as anyone before him. He especially wanted to win for Coach Stevenson. Coach was the man who had taught him so much about hockey and life.

Yet after two periods, the Hurricanes were losing by two goals. During the final intermission, Mario told his coach not to worry. He would take care of things. And so he did, scoring three goals in the final period. It was just enough to win. But people were wondering: could Mario, *would* Mario, do more than just enough if he made it to junior? Could he ever be as good as Lafleur? Mario had his own thoughts on the matter. He knew he would be better.

CHAPTER FOUR

Junior Pro

From age 14 to 15, Mario Lemieux breezed through Quebec's Midget Triple A hockey league, playing for the Montreal Concordia. While he had won every award that he could have won as a younger peewee and bantam player, Mario answered the people who doubted him, who said he'd never make it with the bigger kids, by breaking a midget record: he scored 62 goals in 40 games, and was the league's top scorer.

He also answered the critics who said he didn't have enough heart and desire. In the last minute of a tied play-off game, an opposing player whacked his stick down on Lemieux's hand, cutting it open. The team doctor told Mario to take off his uniform and head for the showers — his injury was too serious to continue playing. Mario listened, then showed how strong his will could be. He told the doctor he was going to play whether the doctor liked it or not. And with only one good hand, he set up the game winner in overtime.

Major Junior League hockey is the most common path towards the NHL. It is a highly competitive league where future NHLers learn how to compete at a high skill level while the eyes of NHL scouts look on and evaluate these young hockey players. In junior hockey, as in the pros, players are selected from the lower leagues through a draft system. Mario knew he was going to be drafted early, but he wanted more. He wanted to be taken Number One.

In the spring of 1981, Mario enrolled in a hockey school at the University of Montreal. While he wasn't the best player on the ice, one man watching from the stands thought Mario was good. In fact, he thought Mario was going to be great. And this man was in a position to know.

Bob Perno was the Quebec partner of Gus Badali, who represented Wayne Gretzky, now a superstar with the Edmonton Oilers. A few years earlier, Perno had read Scotty Bowman's remarks in a Montreal newspaper about how this 12-year-old kid named Mario Lemieux was the best prospect Bowman had ever seen. Bowman was not in the habit of giving such gushing praise, so Perno took his scissors and clipped the article out of the paper. He put it in his file of "Things To Keep An Eye On." And now at this hockey school, he had his eyes very much on Mario Lemieux.

Mario stood almost six feet (180 cm) tall and had gained weight. He looked much more solid out there on the ice. His new size complemented his amazing ability to see the ice as if he was floating above it, while those magic hands of his could make amazing things happen with the puck.

"I saw great things in him the first day I saw him," Bob Perno said later. "That night, I called [my partner] Gus and said 'This guy is good. This guy is another

Wayne.' He said, 'Don't even say that.' I said, 'But he's another Wayne, only bigger.'"

Mario Lemieux and his family knew that getting an agent was going to be the easy part for their boy. What agent in his right mind wouldn't want a percentage of the fortune Mario Lemieux was going to earn playing pro hockey? Bob Perno knew that other agents were trying to woo Mario and his family, but he had something that no other agent had. Perno's partner represented Wayne Gretzky, and Mario Lemieux knew what that could mean. Big money and the big time. But he wanted to make sure.

"If I break all the Quebec junior scoring records and become the number one junior player in the world," asked Mario, "how much money do you think you could get me?"

This was unusual talk from a 15-year-old, but now Bob Perno knew that Mario was no ordinary kid on or off the ice. Perno told him that if he did everything he said and was also the first pick in the NHL draft, he could get young Mario one million dollars. It was the magic number. Mario shook Perno's hand. He had an agent. Now he had to go out and keep his promises.

Mario was selected first overall in the 1981 Quebec junior draft by the Laval Voisins, who were tempted to take another future NHL star, Sylvain Turgeon, but instead chose Mario as their savior. The Voisins (Neighbors), from a northern suburb of Montreal, certainly needed someone like Mario, because they weren't very good. The year before Mario's arrival, they had finished with the worst record in the league: 21 wins, 2 ties, and 49 losses. Even so, Mario was pumped. He told his agent Perno, and the team's owner, Claude Fournel, that Laval's worries were over. He was going to lead the team to the Stanley Cup of junior hockey, the Memorial Cup. It was a bold promise.

As he prepared to begin his first season in the Major Junior League, the 16 year old now stood six feet (180 cm) tall and weighed 200 pounds (91 kg). He had carved out a new identity for himself by changing his jersey number. Until now, Mario had worn number 27 in honor of his older brother Alain. When he entered the junior ranks, his agent told him he had to be his own man, and that meant his own number. Lemieux, wanting to be the best, said he would wear number 99, after his new hero, Wayne Gretzky. Mario's agent gently told him that this might seem a little too aggressive, so they decided on a compromise. They would turn the 99 upside down, and Mario would become number 66.

In his first year with Laval, Mario scored 30 goals and 66 assists in 64 games, or a point and half a game. However, the Quebec Major Junior League was a high scoring one, and to notch 96 points was seen by some critics as nothing special, even if Mario did help the Voisins better their record to 30-33-1.

Mario's 96 points were the highest in the league of all the rookies playing that season, and Mario was sure that he would win the Rookie-of-the-Year Award. After all, one of his promises to himself and his agent was that he would be the best in the league. Yet, the player he had beaten out as the Number One pick, Sylvain Turgeon, was given that honor. As Pierrette Lemieux burst into tears, Mario was reeling, as if he had been hit with a heavy body check. Turgeon, who played for the Hull Olympiques, had 23 points less than Lemieux. How could this be?

It was Mario's first real lesson that being the best meant more than scoring the most points. And that the world wasn't always a fair place. Many people thought Mario deserved the award, but that he didn't get it because the other owners didn't like Claude Fournel, the owner of Mario's team. So they voted for Turgeon to get even with Fournel, and Mario got caught in the middle. The only thing that Mario could do was to promise to come back even harder the next season, and show the other managers and owners how wrong they had been.

Mario was so determined to be the best that he even quit school to devote all of his time to hockey. He was going on 17 years old, and he had a Grade Ten education. His agent, Perno, warned him that a career in hockey wasn't a sure thing. What if he got injured, and could never play again? Wayne Gretzky, who was now Mario's friend, sent word that education was important, but Mario was not to be moved. Besides, his parents supported him in this huge decision. So, showing a force of will that some called stubbornness, Mario dropped out of high school.

His agent worried about Mario's future, so Perno convinced him to do something that would help Lemieux both in hockey and in life: learn English. It's difficult to believe when you hear him speak, but once upon a time Mario could barely speak English. Montreal is a bilingual city, where many people can switch from French to English or English to French as easily as they breathe. However, there is a saying in Canada that the English and the French are "two solitudes," who live together, but separately. Mario Lemieux's childhood was proof of this. He lived in French, he went to school in French, and he played hockey in French. But he knew that if he was going to make it in the NHL, and if he was going to make lots of money selling hockey gear and other products on TV, then he had to speak English. So he enrolled in an intensive English course.

That 1982–83 season, it seemed as if Mario Lemieux's decision to quit school had paid off. His points almost doubled, with his goal total soaring to 84, and his assist total to 100, for a staggering 184 points in 66 games. However, a new kid on the ice by the name of Pat LaFontaine did even better than Mario. LaFontaine, an American playing for the Verdun Jr. Canadiens, beat Lemieux's great season by scoring 104 goals and 130 assists in 70 games. Mario had led his team to the best record in the league at 53 wins and 17 losses, but the Voisins sputtered in the playoffs. The team that everyone expected to win the Quebec League and head off to the Memorial Cup was eliminated in the semifinals by a team that had finished 26 points behind them in the regular season. Mario was devastated. Showing both his hatred for losing and his youthful immaturity, Mario made a mistake that haunted him for years…he blamed the loss on his participation in the World Junior Championships that had taken place earlier that season. He blamed Canada.

CHAPTER FIVE

Mario vs. Canada

At the end of each December, the best junior hockey players from around the world come together in the World Junior Championships. Players compete hard with each other to be chosen to wear the jersey bearing their national colors. They know that it's an honor to represent their country, and, with skill and little bit of luck, to win a medal. They also know that the eyes of the professional hockey world are glued to the World Juniors, as they're called. Every NHL team wants to see who is the best in this gathering of international excellence.

Players have to make sacrifices, though. Not only do they miss spending the holiday season with their families, they also have to interrupt their regular junior hockey season. For most of them, it's a sacrifice which they can live with. Especially if it means they can come home with a gold medal, and even better chances for a professional career.

In December 1982, Mario Lemieux was thrilled to be chosen for Team Canada to go to the 1983 World Juniors (which begins in December and ends in January, so it takes the end year as its date). Expectations were high for the Canadians. The year before, a team coached by future NHL coaches Dave King and Mike Keenan had won the gold medal. That win was huge because it was the first time since 1961, when the Trail (British Columbia) Smoke Eaters beat the Soviets for gold, that any Canadian team had done the same. Since Canada likes to think of itself as being the best hockey-playing nation in the world, Mario's Team Canada was expected to go to Leningrad, in the still-Communist Soviet Union, and bring back a glittering gold medal. And Canadians expected Mario Lemieux to make sure of it.

Mario was excited and a little nervous. He had promised his agent that he would break junior records in Quebec, but so far, he had not. He said he would take his junior team to the Memorial Cup, and again, he had not. Still, he had another year and a half of junior hockey left. It was nice to know that he was achieving one of his goals by representing Canada against the best of the world. He was confident that he would make the world notice.

His Team Canada coach, Dave King, wasn't so sure. King, a keen student of the game, insisted that anyone who played for him played a complete hockey game. You worked flat out at both ends of the ice, and you didn't let up until you hit the bench after your shift. King had heard the criticisms of Mario — that he skated too slowly; that he played without emotion; that the concept of back-checking seemed as foreign to him as English often did. King was waiting to be impressed.

Mario had heard the criticisms before, and he would hear them for years to come. He would say that because he was bigger, he seemed to be skating slower. Other players, who tried to catch him once he'd blown by them, said that this was indeed true, Mario was as fast as they come. Mario said that he had the same desire to win as any other player, but because he wasn't running all over the ice, it might seem that he was relaxing. He saw the ice differently, and picked his moments to strike. And as he once told his agent, Bob Perno, his sense of defense was offense: if he had the puck for 75% of the game, wasn't that defense enough?

Unfortunately for Mario, Dave King wanted to see Lemieux prove that he belonged. When he didn't see Mario on fire, he did something to the young Quebec superstar-in-waiting that no one had ever done before. He put Mario on the fourth line.

Lemieux was as angry as he had ever been. And he was sore: he had an injured knee, one that he'd banged up in this very tournament. As he sat on the bench, watching other players out there on the ice where he should be, he got even angrier. At night, he tossed and turned in his hotel room bed, which was far too short for his frame — now almost 6'4'' (190 cm). He hated the Soviet Union, and he missed home. He hated Dave King, and he missed his Quebec team. When Canada lost 7-3 to the Soviets, they went home with the bronze medal and not the gold, which stayed in the USSR. And Mario went home with a promise. He would never play in the World Juniors again.

For the rest of his junior season, Mario fumed about his mistake in going to Leningrad. While he was gone, his Quebec Major Junior scoring rival Pat LaFontaine used

Mario's time at the World Juniors to lock up the scoring championship. This trip had cost Mario far more than he could have imagined. He had been injured, he was jet-lagged, he had been humiliated, and now he had lost the chance to keep one of his promises to win a scoring title, a promise that could make or break his future. Finally, the devastating loss in the playoffs capped a terrible year. Unsure of what went so horribly wrong, Mario blamed his participation at the World Juniors. So when Team Canada came calling again the following December to invite Mario to the 1984 World Juniors, his reply was short and to the point: "No."

He was in his last year of junior hockey. He still had to break Guy Lafleur's astonishing record of 130 goals, and he wanted to break Pierre Larouche's record of 251 points. And he still had to take his team to the Memorial Cup. If he went to play in the World Championships in Sweden, he could do further damage to his goals, and this year, his chance of accomplishing them looked better than ever.

Mario was having his best season so far. Though Lafleur had set his record in a 62-game season, Lemieux had the luxury of eight more games. After the first 22 games of the 1983–84 campaign, he had 40 goals, the same number Lafleur had after the same number of games. Better still, he had 94 points, or more than four points a game. He was hot.

This made Team Canada want him even more. Everyone tried to talk him into coming to Sweden: things would be different this year, they said. Dave King was no longer the coach, and Mario was an even better player. Mario listened, and again he said no.

The Quebec Junior Hockey League bosses were furious. They huddled in meetings, and came up with a solution. If Mario wouldn't act in the best interests of his league, his province, and his country, then they wouldn't let him play at all. If he wanted to stay home so he could play in the four games he would miss if he went to Sweden, the League would take its sweet revenge by suspending him — for four games.

Mario was furious. He didn't feel that anybody should have the right to force him to play at the Worlds. It was his personal decision. Though he was just 17 years old, Mario asked the Quebec Supreme Court to stop the league from making him do something he felt would damage his career. The league was shocked. The people of Quebec were shocked. The people of Canada were shocked. The judge, however, was not.

He ruled that Mario was under contract to play for the Laval Voisins, and that was that. He was not under contract to go jetting off to play for Team Canada. Even so, the judge echoed the sentiments of many Canadians when he said that Mario should realize that he was a junior professional and must make some sacrifices. But Mario Lemieux had won his point, even if he had lost the support and good will of many people who thought he was selfish. It was a damaging image of him that would last many years.

While Team Canada finished out of the medals at the

World Juniors, Mario was working on setting his records in the Quebec league. In those four games that he otherwise would have missed if he had played for his country, he scored two goals and added nine assists. And he continued scorching the ice.

He would beat Pierre Larouche's record of 252 points with five games left in the season. However, with only one game left, Mario was still three short of the record he most wanted to beat: those 130 goals of his boyhood idol Guy Lafleur. Playing against another Montreal suburban team, Longueuil, and with Wayne Gretzky watching in the stands, Mario was under huge pressure. Would he crack?

With his promise to be the best riding on his shoulders, and the raucous crowd waiting to make him their hero, Mario gave notice early that he was serious scoring his first goal 43 seconds into the game, then his second a minute and 20 seconds later. At 1:18 of the second period, he tied Lafleur's record. Six minutes later, he broke it. The 400 fans in the arena went wild, but Mario wasn't finished. He added two more goals and five assists for an 11 point "last hurrah." He had scored 133 goals and added 149 assists for an astonishing 282 points. He was indeed the best. He had only one promise left to fulfill: win the Memorial Cup.

The Memorial Cup is the championship trophy of junior hockey. The tournament was created in 1919, in memory of the great young players who were killed in World War I. Each year, the champions of the QMJHL, the Ontario Hockey League (OHL), the Western Hockey League (WHL), and the team that is hosting the tournament meet in a round robin competition. This means that the teams all play each other, and whichever two teams have the best record at the end, play for the Memorial Cup.

Mario Lemieux had promised that he would bring the Cup to Laval when he first joined the team in 1981. Now, in the spring of 1984, he was getting his last chance to make good on one of his key promises, both to his team, and to himself.

Things looked good for Laval in the Quebec playoffs to get to the Cup, mainly because Mario was a scoring machine: 29 goals and 23 assists in 14 games. It was another league record. And Laval easily won the championship of Quebec. Now they were going to the Memorial Cup in Kitchener, Ontario.

People came from all over the hockey world to see how Mario Lemieux would perform under tough playoff pressure. They were people like NHL general managers, who could ensure that Mario would keep another of his promises and go first in the NHL draft that summer. Lemieux had already rewritten the Quebec junior hockey record books, but there were still people who thought he didn't have enough heart. Since Laval didn't play games outside of Quebec, many people from the Canadian west and the United States hadn't seen Mario yet, but they had heard about his greatness. They were expecting a superhero.

Instead, they got a phantom. In the first game against

Kitchener, Mario was held to no points, as his team was pasted 8-2. Afterward, the Laval coach tried to blame Mario for doing nothing, and the players took Mario's side. A mutiny was brewing, especially when Mario boldly told a reporter that the coach "should keep his mouth shut."

In the second game, against Ottawa, Mario managed a goal and an assist, but his team still lost 6-5. They had to win their next game against Kamloops if they hoped to stay alive in the tournament, let alone take home the Cup. Mario was troubled. He was finding that the Memorial Cup was the toughest hockey he had ever played. The players on the western teams were bigger and hard to go around. They played a different kind of hockey, a more physical kind, and Mario was frustrated.

So much so that Mario only managed an assist against Kamloops. The westerners beat Laval and Mario 4-3. It was over. Mario would not win the Memorial Cup now, or ever. After averaging three or four points a game all season, he could only notch three in three games. The people who doubted him said, "See? Told you so."

Mario's agent, Bob Perno, tried to figure out what happened. "I don't think Mario knew what was wrong. He'd played nearly 100 games [that season] at a super-natural pace; maybe he was just worn out. It was as close as he ever came to failure."

Mario took some consolation by winning the award as the best junior player in Canada, the same country for whom he refused to play in the World Junior Championships. His decision had allowed him to smash the Quebec record books, but, as if in revenge, the Canadian hockey gods embarrassed him in the Memorial Cup. He knew how good he was, and had high hopes of going first in the NHL amateur draft in a few weeks time. He felt he had worked hard to get to this point, and now he wanted his reward. There was no doubt that he would be picked to play pro hockey. The question was did the people who did the picking think he was as good as he knew himself to be?

CHAPTER SIX

Number One?

Every June, promising junior hockey players gather in an NHL arena and endure a process a bit like picking teams for schoolyard shinny. It's called the NHL Entry Draft and getting picked early can make your career, or it can put so much pressure on you that you fail miserably. The NHL is littered with "first round busts" — players who were picked in the first round, when each NHL team takes the player they want most, if he's still available. Getting picked late — or worse, not at all — can make some players work harder, as the player tries to show everyone that the people doing the selecting were wrong. It can also make some tough young hockey players cry like babies. They know they might never make it to the NHL, might never live the dream they've worked all their lives to live.

In the summer of 1984, Mario Lemieux had no such worries. Everyone said he was going to be picked high in the first round, but Mario wanted to be picked Number One overall, just like he was in junior hockey. And this time, if he were picked Number One, he could make his agent keep a promise to him, the one that would make young Mario a millionaire.

Mario's best shot of being the Number One pick overall would come if the Pittsburgh Penguins held on to their first overall pick. In the NHL, the team that finished last in the standings gets to pick first at the draft. In this way, teams that are bad have a chance of selecting a budding young superstar who can help them improve. Teams with the first pick also know that they have something very valuable to trade away. They can give their first round pick to another NHL team in exchange for players who have already proven they can play at the highest level in the world.

In the summer of 1984, the Pittsburgh Penguins were more than living up to their namesake — a bird that lives on ice but can't fly. All that the hockey team seemed good at was losing. The Penguins had waddled to 16 wins, 6 ties, and 58 losses, giving them a sorry points total of 38 — last in the league. It was their worst season since they came into the NHL as an expansion team in 1967.

The only good thing that came out of their disastrous season was the fact that they had the Number One draft pick. Indeed, the Penguins had made sure of that by trading away their best defenseman, Randy Carlyle, to Winnipeg, and by sending their young netminder Roberto Romano to the minors, to be replaced with a goalie who let in an average of six goals a game. The Penguins lost 15 of their final 18 games and won the right to pick first.

The Penguins badly needed a player like Mario and Mario seemed to want to play for a team like Pittsburgh. He wanted to play in the United States. He wanted a team that wasn't too good, one like his Laval junior team, that he could remake single-handedly.

Pittsburgh's General Manager Eddie Johnston was happy to give Mario Lemieux his wish. He had managed to convince the team's owner, Edward De Bartolo, that Mario Lemieux was the guy who could save the franchise in Pittsburgh. The woeful Penguins were averaging 6700 fans a night, and if things didn't change soon, the team would have to move.

Other teams didn't make it easy for Eddie Johnston, a former NHL goalie. Minnesota's GM Lou Nanne said that Mario was the type of player "you could build a franchise around." He offered a huge deal in return for Mario: all twelve of the Minnesota North Star's draft picks in exchange for Mario. Johnston said no. The Quebec Nordiques offered Johnston their prized trio of Stastny brothers, Marion, Peter, and Anton, but again Johnston said no.

Johnston had no time for all the "Mario Doubters." He was positive that Mario Lemieux was going to come into the NHL and be a star from the very first game. "You look at the guys who have been great players in the league, but he's broken every record they have," said Johnston. "We need that big, dominant guy, and this guy's presence is felt. He's got great skills. It's 99.9% [certain] this guy can come in [to the NHL]. He's the best player in the country."

The Penguins were so keen to get Mario Lemieux in their black and gold jersey that they even began talking contract before they had picked him. This was fine with Mario. He wanted that $1 million that his agent Perno had promised to get him a few years earlier.

While Pittsburgh wanted to sign Mario and were willing to pay him well, they felt $1 million for a player who had yet to play a minute at the NHL level was too risky, especially since Mario had failed to do anything in the Memorial Cup. To be sure, Mario Lemieux was a great player, and one day might even be among the very best in the NHL. They thought $700,000 was a fair deal.

Mario disagreed. The Penguins were already using his image to sign up season ticket holders for the new season. They had plunked a picture of the jersey he would wear as a Penguin — Number 66 — on their promotional material. The Penguins were using him to sell tickets, but they wouldn't pay him what he felt he was worth. Mario was insulted.

Aside from the fact that the 1984 NHL Entry Draft featured Mario Lemieux, it was also in Montreal, Mario's hometown. The city was buzzing: all of hockey-loving Montreal wanted to see Mario, their Mario, be chosen Number One. Since this was also the first time that the draft was going to be televised live throughout Canada, in English and French, by the CBC, hockey fans across the country were going to be able to watch the spectacle. Just so US viewers weren't deprived, the Penguins had arranged for a live video feed to link the draft at the Montreal Forum to the arena in Pittsburgh, known to everyone as the Igloo. They had even sold 8,000 tickets for the event — which was 1300 people more than usual-ly came to the Igloo to watch the Penguins play. The city of Pittsburgh was buzzing too.

And Mario was buzzing with anger. On June 8, the night before the draft, his agent and the Penguins were behaving like old enemies. Back and forth they had gone, arguing over money. The Penguins wouldn't budge from $700,000; Mario wouldn't budge from $1 million. He even took his cause to the Montreal newspapers, which was unusual for him. Mario didn't court the media, but he did speak plainly when he had something to say. "The Penguins won't make me bend," is what he told the French press, and all of Montreal read it.

Finally, the Penguins made a concession. They offered $760,000. Mario listened as his agent told him the news but felt it was still an insult to his talent, considering the riches which that talent would bring to Pittsburgh. So he said no — $760,000 was still quite a bit short of $1 million. To prove his point, he said he was going golfing in the morning instead of going to the draft.

His parents were upset, especially his mother Pierrette. All his life she had nurtured his hockey talents, from the snow-covered living-room floor all the way to the Memorial Cup. She was so looking forward to the moment when his name would ring out in the historic Montreal Forum, a place that had seen some of the greatest players in hockey history. That moment was as much hers as it was his.

Mario's agent also pleaded with him to reconsider. He pointed out that Mario's refusal to play for Canada six months earlier had already given him a bad image in many people's minds. What would they think if he refused to go to the draft?

Mario decided that for the sake of his family and his

image, he would go to the draft. His agent got him there 45 minutes early, in case Pittsburgh decided to cave in. They did not. When Eddie Johnston, a Montreal native, stood at the podium and announced in French that the Penguins took "le soixante-six (the [number] sixty-six), Mario Lemieux!" everyone cheered, waiting for Mario to come down to the Pittsburgh table and pull on a Penguins jersey, as both tradition and manners dictated. Instead, Mario did nothing.

Shock rippled through the Forum. A draft pick refusing to go down and accept the honor of playing in the NHL was unheard of. With the media rushing to Mario's seat in the stands, Eddie Johnston called Mario's name again. Mario stood up, waved to the crowd, and sat back down. People in the Forum started to boo; people watching on TV at the Pittsburgh Igloo began to boo as well. Mario's mother was crying.

The Penguins sent representatives up to try to drag Mario down to pull on a Pittsburgh jersey, but he would not budge. "Don't tell me what to do when you won't pay me what I'm worth," Mario told the Pittsburgh man, who retreated in fury. Around them, the draft continued. Montreal picked Patrick Roy with the 51st pick; Brett Hull was selected 117th by the St. Louis Blues; Luc Robitaille went 171st. (All three demonstrating that being picked high is a guarantee of nothing.) Mario wasn't around to see these future NHL stars joyfully descend from the stands and put on their new team jerseys. He had left the building. Another image disaster was on the horizon.

The newspapers jumped on it right away. "Lemieux Behaving Like a Petulant Prima Donna," said Toronto's *Globe & Mail*, comparing Mario to a spoiled, vain opera singer. "Mario Snub a Tasteless Act" said the Montreal *Gazette*. Only in the French newspapers did Mario get any sympathy. They understood that he was a Francophone (French-speaking Canadian) who would not be bullied by the English, or the Americans. They were proud of him. But they did not have a lot of company.

Two weeks later, after everyone had calmed down, a spirit of compromise was in the air. Mario wanted to play in the NHL; the Penguins wanted him to play for them. So the two sides crafted a deal in which Mario would receive $700,000 over two years, with a rumored $150,000 signing bonus. If he played very, very well, then other bonuses would kick in, and he could make his million dollars.

Everyone was happy, and the anger vanished into the blue summer skies. Mario bought his father a new red Pontiac Parisienne to replace the old rust bucket that had driven him to games on cold winter mornings. Then he settled back to enjoy the rest of the summer with his new girlfriend, Nathalie Asselin. He was 18 years old, and about to enter the NHL. Life was good. Meanwhile, the Penguins and the public had not forgotten the trouble it took to get Mario into a Pittsburgh jersey. They were expecting very big things.

CHAPTER SEVEN

The Big Time

Every September, NHL teams gather to hold training camp to see who will be on the team when the season begins in October. For established players, training camp is a bit like coming back to school after a great summer. You get to see all your friends and trade stories about what you did on your vacation. You know that your place in the school is secure, and you're looking forward to a great year.

For role players, whom management considers replaceable, training camp is a test to see if they will keep their jobs. It can be a struggle, and at any time during camp, you can be "cut," and sent home with your kit bag as if you've been expelled from school.

For rookies, training camp is like being the new kid at school. All the other kids are curious to see what kind of stuff you're made of, and they will let you know loud and clear if they think that you don't have the right stuff. Rookies have to earn the respect of everyone, and no one makes it easy for them.

The veteran Pittsburgh Penguins players were keen to see this new kid, Mario Lemieux. Unless they had been sleeping for the past three months, they couldn't have missed all the hype around him, with headlines in the Pittsburgh papers saying things like "Glory Days Ahead" when Lemieux was picked Number One.

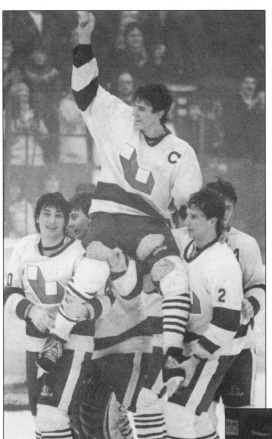

Mario's Laval Voisins teammates of the Quebec Major Junior Hockey League (QMJHL) hoist him on their shoulders in celebration of Mario's breaking Guy Lafleur's record of 130 goals in a season. Mario finished the 1983/84 season with a staggering 133 goals and 149 assists.

The Laval Voisins would win the QMJHL Championships in 1984 but fail to capture the Memorial Cup—one of the few prizes to elude Mario's grasp.

Mario debuts with the Pittsburgh Penguins in a pre-season all-rookie game. *Inset:* The 1st overall draft pick works out at his first NHL training camp.

Mario digs against the Chicago Blackhawks during the 1992 Stanley Cup Finals. Mario would lead the Penguins to their second consecutive championship.

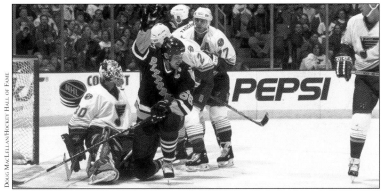

Finding a way to score, Mario completes a hat trick in December 1996 against the St. Louis Blues.

Mario celebrates the 1992 Stanley Cup repeat.

Representing
Canada at the
1987 Canada Cup

Perhaps the two most gifted
hockey players ever to have
ever laced up skates—Wayne
Gretzky and Mario Lemieux
face each other at the NHL
All-Star Game.

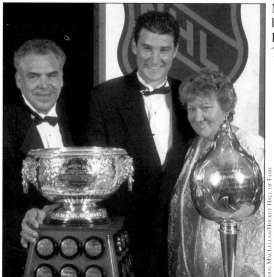

Mario poses with his parents, the Art Ross and the Hart Trophy in 1996.

Lemieux accepts the Masterton, Art Ross, and Hart Trophies in 1993.

April 23, 1997: In an emotional farewell, Mario acknowledges the fans after his final game.

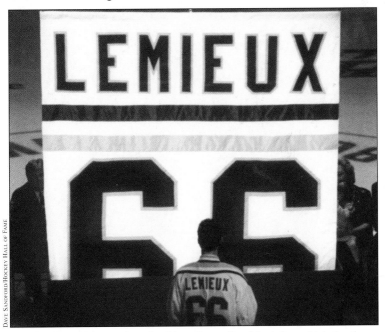

The famous 66 jersey is retired just days after Mario's rapid induction into the Hockey Hall of Fame.

After a nearly four-year hiatus, Mario returned as player/owner on December 27, 2000. In just 43 games, Mario scores 35 goals and 41 assists for a sublime 1.77 points per game average. It's an astonishing feat for any player, let alone one who had been out of the game for such a long period.

Sure, the Penguins knew that their previous season was the stuff of a bad dream, but it was a little insulting to be told that one 18-year-old kid — who had never played a game in the NHL — was going to lead them to greatness. And when they finally saw the kid up close, they thought they had been victims of a major hoax.

Despite all his natural talent, Mario Lemieux was not exactly a model athlete in his youth. An ideal Mario meal would be a burger and fries, topped off with some crème caramel or chocolate for dessert. Mario and his friends used to cram into his mother's kitchen after playing hockey, and she'd make them whatever fried, greasy, sugary delight they wanted. Despite the junk food, Mario wasn't fat. In fact, he was so thin that his mother used to feed him vitamin and protein supplements to help strengthen him.

Mario was also a stranger to training. He figured that since he played so much hockey, he didn't need to work out in the off-season by lifting weights and running. In fact, he much preferred to have a few beers with his teammates on their way to chat up girls at the local roller rink. And he smoked. Not just the occasional cigarette to seem cool, but half a pack of cigarettes a day!

One of the first drills the Pittsburgh coaches gave the team was a simple weight drill. Lying on his back, each player had to take a barbell weighing 180 pounds (81.8 kg), and lift it into the air ten times. For big strong hockey players, it was supposed to be an easy drill. The players lifted the weights as if they were lifting the Stanley Cup over their heads. Burly tough guy Marty McSorley, who had signed with the Penguins as a free agent in 1982, lifted the barbell with such ease it could have been a hockey stick.

Then came Mario Lemieux's turn. At 6'4'' (190 cm), he was the tallest player on the team. At a bit over 200 pounds (91 kg), he was one of the heaviest, too, but the Penguins had noticed something odd about him. While his legs were strong and muscular from hockey, his upper body looked like it belonged to someone else — the pale, scrawny torso of the average 18-year-old.

Everyone watched as Mario lay down on the bench and gripped the weights. He pumped his arms to shoot the barbell toward the ceiling, but nothing happened. He tried again, and still the weights didn't budge. Now the Penguins were starting to laugh, first one veteran, then another. Then the whole room was roaring as Mario tried to lift the weights — even just a little bit — off the bar which supported them. He couldn't even make the weights move, and the Penguin players were all howling like schoolboys. Here was the guy who was going to save their team and he couldn't even do the most basic of strength drills. What a joke.

The joke would be on them, because what they didn't know — but would soon learn — was that Mario Lemieux doesn't like to be humiliated. When he walked out of that training room, the sharp laughter of his team-mates stabbed him in the heart. He knew that he didn't need to run fast or lift heavy weights to show them what he could do. He would work his magic on the ice.

Everyone in Pittsburgh was expecting great things from Mario. After all, the Penguins had been advertising their savior for months — in their season ticket campaigns, with special events at the Igloo, and with local radio stations even playing 30-second spots talking about Mario's childhood! Pittsburgh's coach Bob Berry warned, "People see a kid like Lemieux and immediately think he's Moses." (He was comparing him to the Biblical hero who led his captive people, the Israelites, out slavery and into the promised land.) If Mario thought he had felt pressure before, he had to readjust his pressure scales. The whole hockey world was watching and waiting for him to make all those promises other people had made about him come true. For him to make miracles.

On October 11, 1984, in the small and noisy Boston Garden, known to everyone as "The Zoo," Mario Lemieux faced off for the first time in a regular season game against the Bruins, who had in recent years been mauling their opponents. Mario stepped onto the ice for his first NHL shift in his first NHL game and almost immediately saw his chance. The Bruins' future Hall-of-Fame defenseman Raymond Bourque attempted a pass in the center of the ice. Mario intercepted the pass with his skate, kicked it up to his stick, and raced towards the Bruins goal.

Now there was nobody between him and Bruins goalie Pete Peeters. It was a situation that Mario had faced many, many times, and he knew exactly what to do. With arms so long that one NHL goalie would compare him to an albatross (a long-winged sea bird), Lemieux faked Peeters to his left, then pulled the puck back the other way. Peeters fell to his knees, as Mario lifted the puck over his shoulder. At 1:41 of the first period, with his first shot, on his first shift, in his first game, Mario Lemieux scored his first NHL goal.

A few nights later, Lemieux made his home debut against the Vancouver Canucks. Nearly 15,000 fans came out to watch the savior do his work, and Mario didn't let them down. Just 18 seconds into the game, Mario charged down the left wing past the Vancouver defenseman. With his keen vision, he saw out of the side of his right eye a Penguin moving into the clear in the slot. And bang! Mario rocketed the puck onto his teammate's stick. The puck was in the net. Mario was a hero already.

Or maybe not. Lemieux didn't score another goal for ten games after his debut in Boston, and the Penguins had a brutal start, with their 6 wins and 1 tie darkened by 14 losses as the season passed the quarter mark and headed to halfway.

After his dazzling beginning, Mario was feeling the heat. "The first ten games were really tough because I felt a lot of pressure on me to do well and maybe I was trying too hard," he said. Like other junior hockey stars before him, Mario was learning that the NHL is a whole different world. "The pace is faster, and the players are bigger, stronger, and smarter, and if you make a mistake, they take advantage of it."

Mario was acknowledging that even he had things to learn about hockey at the NHL level. "In junior hockey, I was criticized a great deal for my defensive play," Mario said. "But in junior, I had the puck much of the time, which seemed to be a good style of defense." Playing with the very best players in the world, Mario began to understand that no one player can dominate the game in the same way he did in junior. He realized that he needed to sharpen up on the defensive aspect of his game now that he was in the pros. "I'm working on defensive play every day here and the coaches are teaching me a great deal. I want to be a good player from one end of the ice to the other and I'll work very hard to be that."

The Penguins, though, had not signed Mario to the largest rookie contract since Wayne Gretzky's in order to watch him play defense. Happily, his offense returned after the ten-game slump. By mid-season, Mario had notched 20 goals and 34 assists in 40 games, and the Penguins were thrilled with what they saw. "Mario has been everything we've expected him to be — and then some," the Pens GM Eddie Johnston said. "If he hadn't missed seven games with a knee injury, he would have another dozen points. There's no doubt who the best NHL rookie is this season."

Others weren't so sure. Mario was constantly compared to Wayne Gretzky, who wore his heart on his sleeve when he played, and who had an impeccable image off the ice. After the Pens lost 6-3 to the Edmonton Oilers in a game where Gretzky scored three goals and an assist, one of Mario's fellow Penguins took a shot at him. "I hope he learned something from the show put on by Wayne Gretzky," said the grumbling teammate. "Gretzky never relaxes on the ice; he's always on the prowl, looking for any little opening. Mario lacks that consistent hunger."

One sportswriter compared Mario's skating style to a massive ocean liner, lazily cruising along on the Atlantic. Canada's hard-headed hockey guru Don Cherry put it more rudely. He called Lemieux "the biggest floater in the NHL."

Mario took those insults and tucked them into his hockey bag, then went on a mission in his first All-Star game. In those days, the All-Star game was not the World versus North America, but was split by conferences, as in the NBA today. So 19-year-old Mario Lemieux of Pittsburgh found himself playing against 23-year-old superstar Wayne Gretzky of Edmonton. It was a matchup that had hockey fans drooling. Mario and Wayne, going head-to-head. Mario seized his chance to impress, scoring two goals and one assist as his side beat Gretzky's. Playing alongside the NHL's brightest stars, Mario Lemieux was named the game's Most Valuable Player.

In a generous gesture, he gave the Chevy Blazer 4x4 truck that he won as MVP to his brother Richard, who was then working as a grocery store clerk. And he gave his tormentor, Don Cherry, a piece of his mind. "That [game]," said Mario, "was for him."

Now that Mario had established his pedigree among the big boys, he played hard for the rest of the season.

Though the Penguins with 53 points finished out of the playoff hunt, they were no longer the worst team in the NHL. Better still, Mario Lemieux had finished the season with 43 goals and 57 assists over 73 games. He had scored 100 points, and in so doing, became only the third rookie in NHL history to accomplish this milestone (Dale Hawerchuk and Peter Stastny were the others). It surprised no one when Mario Lemieux was handed the shining silver Calder Trophy as the NHL's Rookie of the Year. He had answered all of the criticisms against him, and shown that not only could he play in the NHL, he could dominate. He was just 19 years old. And he was just getting started.

CHAPTER EIGHT

Super Mario

After his award-winning rookie season, Mario Lemieux was looking forward to taking his girlfriend Nathalie to Scotland. He could play the other game that he loved best — golf — and unlike in Pittsburgh, he could go out in public without everyone recognizing him. However, after such a fine debut, there would be others who wanted to make alternative travel plans for Mario.

Every April, hockey teams from around the globe meet at a tournament called the World Championships. It is a competition that is supposed to match the best players in the world against each other, but for many NHL players, there is a problem. In April, the NHL playoffs begin and stars on playoff teams cannot go to represent their countries in the Worlds. In the spring of 1985, Mario Lemieux had no such problem, as the Penguins hadn't made it into the playoffs. Yet when the call came for him to go and represent his country in a tournament where Canada had last won a gold medal in 1961, Mario said no.

After a long and impressive rookie season, he was tired and wanted some time to himself. He also remembered what had happened the last time he went to play for Canada. He was not the least bit interested in having it happen again. So, a team of persuaders assembled to try to make Mario change his mind: the powerful hockey agent and lawyer Alan Eagleson; Mario's GM in Pittsburgh, Eddie Johnston; Mario's and Wayne Gretzky's agent, Gus Badali; and even Guy Lafleur, Mario's childhood hero from the Montreal Canadiens.

It was hard to resist their arguments, so Mario did something he almost never did: he changed his mind. Yes, he said, he would go represent Canada in the World Championships.

Once he arrived in Europe, though, a familiar pattern soon emerged. Just like the last time he played in world competition, Mario wasn't impressed by Europe. He wasn't the type of guy who liked to go to museums and art galleries. Instead, Mario's idea of a good time was playing Nintendo, or sleeping. Despite the fact that Prague, where the tournament was held, is one of Europe's oldest and culturally rich cities, Mario was bored. Worse, he had pulled a groin muscle during the NHL season, and once he arrived in what was then Czechoslovakia, the injury flared up. He sat out two games, and watched his team lose to the Soviets. "I've never been hurt very much so it was very difficult to deal with," he said. The truth was, he wanted to go home.

His agent, Bob Perno, tried to talk him out of it. Even though it was three o'clock in the morning Montreal time, Mario's agent was now wide awake and he was angry. Didn't Mario realize that he had already angered many people by the things he had done — or rather, not done? Had he forgotten the bad feeling that he created when he went to court in order to *avoid* playing for his country? Here was his chance to prove he was good guy, a patriot. Did he want to blow that?

Mario replied that he was hurt, and he wanted to go home. So the sly lawyer Alan Eagleson did something to Mario that he would eventually go to jail for doing to other players. He lied to him. Eagleson told Mario that Team Canada wanted him to go home. They didn't need him hanging around like a dark cloud. If golfing in Scotland was more important than playing for his country, then fine, see you later. However, said Eagleson, there was one problem. They couldn't get Mario a flight home for three or four days. He would have to hang around and watch his ex-team try to do their best without him.

Eagleson had not even tried to get a flight home for Mario. Some people call it lying, some people call it "reverse psychology," but whatever you want to call it, the trick worked. After sitting in the stands and watching his team lose 4-2 to the United States, Mario changed his mind yet again. He wanted to play.

The Canadian team that had looked as if it were dead suddenly became came back to life. With Mario back in the lineup, the Canadians knocked off Team Finland, then played the Soviets in a medal round match. The Soviets had smacked down the Canadians 9-1 in the opening round and were licking their lips. No Canadian team had beaten the Soviets at the world championships since 1961. And the Soviets weren't going to let it happen now.

Mario, though was determined. And when he was

determined, there was no stopping him. He scored two of Canada's three goals as they stunned the Soviets 3-1. "It's not every day you get the chance to beat the Russians," Mario said, barely containing his glee. And when the Canadians came home from the tournament with a silver medal, Mario showed how happy he was. It was Canada's best showing in international competition since 1962. "Doing this is the greatest thrill I ever dreamed of," he said. His world had just become much bigger.

Mario's strong play at the Worlds continued when he resumed play in the NHL. Over the next two years, Mario's scoring numbers soared to the heights that people expected. In 1985–86, he notched 48 goals and 93 assists for 141 points. The following year, having played only 63 games due to a knee injury, he scored 54 goals and added 53 assists for 107 points. The Penguins were better too, but after three seasons with Mario, they still had not made the playoffs. And so some people doubted that Mario was the kind of franchise player that Gretzky was, the kind who could lead his team to a championship. That opportunity would soon arrive, as the 1987 Canada Cup approached.

Mario wanted to show all his doubters that he was first rate, and that no one should question his heart. He felt that his talent had not always been shown to its best advantage. Aside from Lemieux and a handful of other players on Pittsburgh, the Penguins were not a team loaded with talent. And the World Championships featured players whose teams did not make it into the playoffs. However, the Canada Cup was different, because it would be Mario's first opportunity to play with the very best, and against the very best, for something that mattered a great deal: the chance to be the best hockey team in the world.

The Canada Cup was able to feature the best teams on the globe because it took place before the NHL season began, in late summer. In this way, the tournament could attract the top players unlike the World Championships which coincided with the NHL playoffs. And for Mario Lemieux, it finally meant the chance to play on the same team as the man to whom everyone compared him: The Great Gretzky.

At first, Canada's fiery coach, Mike Keenan, had his doubts about Mario's desire to win, and used Mario and Gretzky together only on the power play. As the series wore on, injuries forced Keenan to put the two out on the ice together, where their two huge talents could combine into something gigantic. "Mario and I have the same hockey instincts and that made it easy to react to each other," said Gretzky. It was typically modest of Gretzky. He meant they had the same type of genius.

Mario was also reacting to Wayne off the ice. He saw how friendly Wayne was to the media and the fans, and how he led by example. Mario began to realize that he could let people see that he too was easygoing and friendly, and had what it took to be a true champion. Though he had won many personal awards, Mario had yet to win a major team championship. Now he was learning from a master who had already won three Stanley Cups — the most recent coming just a few months earlier when they defeated Philadelphia in seven games.

Mario and Wayne didn't really get a regular chance to play together until the three-game final against the Russians. Canada was heading to the medal round undefeated, with two wins and two ties. And Mario was on fire: he had scored seven goals, and four more in an exhibition series with the Russians. Now he would face them again in the final.

Canada and Russia had always been fierce rivals. Each nation thought itself the best hockey-playing country in the world. In international competition, the Russians had the edge as the Canadian NHL players could not compete in international amateur competitions and the Russians had yet to enter the NHL in large numbers as they do today. In 1972, for the very first time, Canada's professional hockey players were allowed to compete against the best that the Russians had to offer. In a thrilling roller coaster ride of an eight-game series, Canada won the right to call themselves the best in the very last minute of the very last game. After that, the rivalry between the two countries heated up to scorching.

Montreal was the scene of Game 1 of the Canada Cup. The Forum, which had seen excitement in its time, was ready to explode. The Russians, however, spoiled the party with a goal in overtime to beat the Canadians 6-5. Mario Lemieux didn't score any goals in that game, but he did manage two assists. And he was waiting to get even.

The next two games were in Hamilton, Ontario. In the first, Mario and Gretzky worked magic, with Mario scoring the last three of Canada's goals, and Gretzky assisting on every one. The most exciting goal came at ten minutes into the second overtime, with the score tied at five, and the crowd on the edge of their seats. Mario converted a beautiful Gretzky pass into the game winner, and the hockey world had a new hero. Now the series was tied, with one game left. The question hung in the air. Did Mario have it in him to be a superhero?

In the final contest, the game was again tied at five. The fans at Copps Coliseum wondered if their hearts could stand another overtime. With less than two minutes on the clock, Mario hadn't scored a goal.

With the face-off in the Canadian zone, and Wayne and Mario on the ice, the tension mounted. Could they save hockey glory for Canada? The puck popped back to the Soviet defenseman Igor Kravchuk on the boards, and Mario Lemieux went after it. His long reach worked to his advantage, and he poked the puck loose and into the clear for Gretzky. Together, the two of them raced down the ice, joined by defenseman Larry Murphy in a three-on-two rush.

The fans stood and screamed as Gretzky crossed the Soviet blue line. Larry Murphy moved toward the Soviet net, taking one defenseman with him. Gretzky kept skating along the boards, pulling the other Soviet d-man towards him. Which left Mario in the open — a very dangerous place for him to be.

Suddenly, Gretzky fed a perfect pass to Mario, right on the tape. And there was nothing in front of him but a Soviet goalie. Mario picked the top corner over the goalie's glove and fired a rocket into it. Mario and Team Canada had just won the Canada Cup.

Mario was overjoyed, not least because he had set a new Canada Cup record for goal scorers with 11 goals (and seven assists). What made him even happier was the respect he had won from the hockey people who had doubted him. He had shown the world that he could play at the highest level of the game.

"No one can ever question Mario's character to me now. He dug down very deep!" said his coach, Mike Keenan. Mario knew that he had. "What can be a greater thrill than scoring the two winning goals against the Russians?" he asked. "I think I have answered some questions about me in this tournament."

He had indeed. He was among the best in the world, "second only to Gretzky," they said. In order to be truly the best, Mario had to do what Gretzky had done three times: win the Stanley Cup. And on that journey, Mario's character would be tested more than he ever could have imagined.

CHAPTER NINE

One Step Forward, Two Steps Back

Mario's success in the Canada Cup elevated his game to a new level. "Just being with all those terrific players was an inspiration," he said. "I'm sure that was when I really reached the peak of my game." And what a peak it was. Before he had been great, now he was Super Mario.

In the 1987-88 season, Mario seemed to win everything. At the NHL awards banquet at the end of the season, he took home the Hart Trophy as the league's most valuable player. He had already been named the MVP of the NHL All-Star game in St. Louis, scoring a record six points (three goals and three assists), including the game-winning goal in overtime. He was named Dodge NHL Performer of the Year. He won the Lester B. Pearson Award (named for the late Prime Minister of Canada) as the NHL's outstanding player, "selected by members of the NHL Players' Association."

It was a sweet honor, for it meant that Mario's fellow players had voted him the best. But the sweetest award of all was the Art Ross Trophy, given to the NHL's top point scorer. Mario had achieved a staggering 70 goals and 98 assists for 168 points. It was 19 points better than Wayne Gretzky's total, and for the first time in seven seasons, someone other than Gretzky would be taking home the Ross. Mario was king.

Or not quite. He still had his critics, and they weren't convinced of anything. They argued that Mario had won the scoring title only because Gretzky had played fewer games, sidelined with a knee injury. But far more importantly, the Penguins, even with Mario's leadership, didn't even make the playoffs. The Oilers, led by Gretzky, won their fourth Stanley Cup. Wayne was still the best. Yet even the best are not safe.

That summer, the Oilers shocked the hockey world when they traded Wayne Gretzky to the Los Angeles Kings. People in Canada cried in the streets and demanded that the government do something to save a "national treasure." Mario, however, was delighted. Gretzky was going to Hollywood, a place where you could become rich and famous. When Gretzky signed an eight-year 20 million dollar deal with the Kings, Mario knew that he was going to get much richer himself. He had just won the scoring title, and he was only 22 years old. He had replaced his Canadian agent, Bob Perno, with Pittsburgh-based Tom Reich. And if Wayne was worth more than $2 million a season, then Mario would be up there, too.

Not only did Mario have a new agent, he had a new coach and a new general manager. All this newness wasn't good. His friend Eddie Johnston was gone as GM and had been replaced by former Chicago Blackhawks' Hall-of-Fame goalie Tony Esposito. The new coach was a former NHL journeyman forward, Gene Ubriaco, who first made it out of the minors and into the pro leagues in 1967, with the Penguins. Ubriaco had never coached in the NHL, but the year before had coached the American Hockey League's Baltimore Skipjacks to an awful record of 13-58-9. He had a habit of giving players nicknames, and he called Mario "Ace." Mario hated it.

Mario didn't like Tony Esposito, whom everyone suspected had been hired because he was a friend of the team's owner. Same with the coach. The first sign of a trouble arrived when astonishing news came out of Montreal. Mario's boyhood idol, Guy Lafleur, wanted to come out of retirement. Even better, he wanted to play with Mario, who was thrilled at the idea of racing down the ice with his childhood hero as his teammate. Yet when Lafleur called the Penguins to see if they wanted him, Tony Esposito ignored him. "He didn't phone back," said Lafleur. "He never really pursued it." So "The Flower" signed with the New York Rangers instead, and Mario was greatly disappointed.

He was even more disappointed when it came time to negotiate his new contract. He had shown the world that he was up there in the stars with Gretzky, and Gretzky was making a fortune. Tony Esposito didn't share Mario's opinion of his worth, and the contract talks went nowhere. Mario set a November deadline, but that came and went. In a game against the New York Rangers that month, Pittsburgh fans started to chant "Sign Lemieux!" over and over. Mario had scored five points, and the fans knew that if Gretzky could be traded, so could Mario.

Finally, on November 30, 1988, both sides reached an agreement: Mario would sign a one-year contract for $1.9 million dollars in Canadian money. Mario would have to negotiate his contract all over again the next year, but at least he was free now to concentrate on hockey.

Though he missed a few games with injuries, Mario went on a scoring tear. Indeed, on New Year's Eve, he displayed the kind of magic that had never been seen before, and has not been seen since. Playing against the New Jersey Devils, Mario scored in every combination possible: he had a regular-strength goal, a short-handed goal, a power-play goal, a penalty-shot goal, and an empty-net goal. It was amazing.

Mario kept going, and at the end of the season, he had once again beaten Gretzky for the Art Ross Trophy. And this time, Gretzky had not been out for a long stretch with injury. There were no excuses. Mario's staggering 85 goals and 114 assists not only gave him the Ross, but he had also become the greatest scorer in the history of the franchise. The Penguins had even made it into the second round of the playoffs, for the first time since 1983.

In Mario's first NHL playoff appearance, he couldn't lead his team past the second round. Despite an 8 point performance against Philadelphia (five goals and three assists in a 10-7 romp), the Penguins blew a three-games-to-two lead against the Flyers and lost the series. To add to his pain, Mario, whom many thought was the league MVP because he was the top scorer, lost the award to Wayne Gretzky.

The following season, 1989–90, saw even more change for Mario and the Penguins. The team had a new general manager, Craig Patrick, part of the legendary Patrick family. Craig was the grandson and great nephew of one of hockey's most illustrious duos, Lester and Frank Patrick. Craig's father, Lynn Patrick, won a Stanley Cup as a player before achieving success as an NHL executive and ultimately being elected to the Hall of Fame. Before this Lynn, Lester, and Frank Patrick had pioneered pro hockey on the Pacific Coast of North America in the early years of the twentieth century, contributing enormously to developing hockey as it is played today.

The Patrick brothers had invented things that we take for granted: the blue line, the penalty shot, numbers on the back of jerseys, the playoff system, and line changes. Before the Patricks, the same players would play the whole 60-minute game, unless they happened to go off due to injury.

With such strong hockey bloodlines, Craig Patrick wanted to make the Penguins better. He said that the best teams knew how to play defense, and that you couldn't win a Stanley Cup without it. He knew that the Penguins didn't have a scoring problem.

Mario Lemieux, now happier with the new boss, took off on a mission to the stars: he was trying to beat Wayne Gretzky's scoring streak of 51 games. Yet it seemed that nothing was allowed to come easily to Mario, and in February of 1990, the pain in his back was so bad that he had to be fitted with a back brace.

When Mario was a junior hockey player, a team doctor had noticed his weak lower back, and had given him a set of back-strengthening exercises. Mario, who hated any kind of exercise that didn't involve hockey or golf, ignored the doctor's advice. Now he was suffering.

On Valentine's Day 1990, Mario and Penguins faced the Rangers in New York. Mario's streak stood at 46 games, and if only he could hang on, he would beat the record that everyone said was untouchable. But at the end of the second period, his back pain was so bad that he had to take himself out of the game. He couldn't even touch below his knees.

Doctors discovered that Mario had a herniated disk in his lower back. A disk is a hockey puck-like piece of cartilage that is between the vertebral bones in your back. It's harder on the outside and softer in the middle, so if a disk ruptures (or herniates), the softer part spills out of the disk. That herniated part presses on the nerve roots, and the brain interprets the irritation of those nerve roots as if the nearby skin or muscle were injured. That's why, depending on the level of the root, herniated disks cause pain in various parts of the back or leg.

Neither Mario nor the Penguins wanted to attempt back surgery. There was no guarantee that the back surgery would work. Even worse, it could end Mario's career. Everyone was scared.

So the doctors made a deal. Mario would undergo extensive physiotherapy for a month. If, at the end of that time, the pain was no better, then they would have to perform the surgery. Mario went to California to begin a program of strengthening exercises on his lower back, abdomen, and legs. To everyone's relief, he felt better. And the Penguins certainly missed him. They won only one of their 12 games as they fought for a playoff spot. If Mario didn't come back, they would miss the playoffs again.

Mario wanted to help his team, and his back felt better — not perfect, but good enough for him to lace on his skates and go out there to help his team. He also knew that if a big opposing defenseman crunched him against boards, or even if he turned the wrong way, he could damage his back — and his career — forever. He accepted the risk because he missed hockey too much. "I've been itching [to play] for a month and a half now," he said. "It was pretty tough [being out], just watching the team."

Though the doctors had told Mario to take it easy, he knew that he had to go full tilt. It was the last game of the season, and if the Penguins could beat Buffalo, they would make the playoffs. If they lost, they would be out.

Though he had been out for two months, Mario played 25 minutes that game, the most of anyone on the ice. He scored a goal and an assist, and the game went into overtime. The Penguins tried to clear the puck out of their zone, but a Buffalo defenseman stopped it and shot it back toward the Pittsburgh net. The shot fooled the Pens' goalie, Tom Barrasso, and went in. The game was over, and with it, the Penguins' season.

Mario had tried his best to save his team with last minute heroics, but he couldn't do it. He took small comfort that his back didn't scream out in pain. It had been a rough year, but all that was behind him now, and, as the optimistic sports saying goes, there's always next year to be a champion. What Mario couldn't know was that next year was going to be like none he had ever seen.

CHAPTER TEN

Mario and Stanley

The 1990–91 season would be one of glory for Mario, but it certainly didn't begin that way. And for Mario, it didn't begin at all. After the disappointing end to the previous season, Mario did what he usually did in the summer. He went golfing. By the end of June, his terrible back pain was back. And now Mario knew that he had to face the inevitable: if back-strengthening exercises had failed, then surgery would be necessary.

In early July, one of the best surgeons in the US operated on Mario and announced that the operation was a success. Mario was more than happy — he was hoping that he would never have to play with back pain again. By August, he was on his skates for light workouts, and by September, he was playing in exhibition games. But when he woke up one morning while on a Texas road trip, he felt a pain in his back. This pain differed from the one before. It was worse.

Mario flew back to Pittsburgh where he received shocking news. His back was infected and the infection was eating away at his spine. Not only did it cause pain, it could cripple him. The doctors stressed that the infection didn't come from the back surgery, but from a sinus infection that Mario had picked up in September.

Bacteria from the infection wound its way to the scar tissue in his back, and poisoned it.

If there was any good news in all of this, it was that the infection could be cured with medicine designed to fight the bacteria. And it didn't look as if the bacteria had done too much damage. If everything went well, Mario would be playing again in three months. Which would be January 1991.

Three months! That seemed like an eternity to Mario, who had already missed a big chunk of the previous season. He was only 25 years old and at the top of his game, and here he was forced to sit and watch and hope that the pills worked. Three months in the life of a hockey player is a long time. And it could take him even longer to recover things like timing, and speed, and lung capacity. It could ruin his season.

The Penguins, however much they missed him, were making the best of it. GM Patrick had hired University of Wisconsin coaching legend "Badger" Bob Johnson, who had won his nickname after that of the team he coached. The Minnesota native had made his mark by coaching the Wisconsin Badgers to three US national college titles in his 15 years behind the bench. He had also coached the Calgary Flames in the NHL, before taking over USA Hockey.

Under "Badger" Bob's leadership, amateur hockey grew huge in the United States. Johnson was the kind of coach known as a player's coach, which means that he understood and liked players. He wanted to make them feel like equals, and treated them with respect. The players loved him, as it was hard not to. Every day he would come to work and say, "It's a great day for hockey." And he meant it.

GM Patrick also hired the legendary hockey genius Scotty Bowman as director of player development. This job title really meant that Bowman could use his expertise to fine-tune the Penguins' lineup. After all, he had won five Stanley Cups as a coach, and he knew what it took to create the team chemistry to win a championship.

That 1990–91 season, the Penguins drafted a young Czech prospect soon to prove himself to be almost as valuable as Mario. Jaromir Jagr had been the Penguins' first choice in the NHL Entry Draft that June, and they believed the kid would be great. They were so confident that they passed up future stars such as Keith Tkachuk and Martin Brodeur.

The 18-year-old Jagr was excited to be going to Pittsburgh. He was a huge fan of Mario's and had even arrived in Pittsburgh carrying a picture of Mario in his wallet. Jagr had been impressed ever since he had first seen Lemieux play. "It was 1985 and he scored on a breakaway against Russia in the World Championship," Jagr said. "I was sitting on my bed watching on TV. I remember how he went top shelf."

When Jagr came to Pittsburgh, GM Craig Patrick threw a party for the new young star to make him feel welcome. Jagr was nervous. He was only 18 years old in a foreign country, and his English wasn't very good.

Soon he was going to be tested in the best hockey league in the world. Would he be good enough? Would he even survive? His worry was put to rest when, to his total surprise, his hero Mario Lemieux showed up at the party. Not only that, but he came over to offer the young Czech player a warm welcome. "I was in the exact same situation as you are now when I came to Pittsburgh speaking only French and I still remember how hard it was," Lemieux told him. "So don't worry, I know the problems you'll be having, and I know how you're feeling. I'm ready to help you out at any time."

Before too long, people realized that Jagr was doing quite nicely on his own. He was big and strong, and could power people off the puck, then keep it away from them as he made it do amazing things before it found its way into the net. People had also noticed that if you re-arranged the letters of Jagr's first name, Jaromir, they spelled "Mario Jr." It was spooky, but in a very good way. Mario Jr. notched 27 goals and 30 assists in his first season in the big leagues, and was named to the All-Rookie All-Star team.

The Penguins had made other changes as well. With Vezina Trophy winner Tom Barrasso in goal, and smooth-skating ex-Edmonton Oiler champ Paul Coffey on the blue line, they added tough, two-way forward Joey Mullen from Calgary. They also got experience and talent in d-man Larry Murphy, and in a trade with Hartford, picked up forwards Ron Francis and John Cullen, and big Swedish defenseman Ulf Samuelsson. The Pens then imported Bryan Trottier from the New York Islanders, where he had won Stanley Cups. Mark Recchi and Kevin Stevens rounded out the forward lines. The Pens had goaltending, experience, strong defense, grit, and fire-power, lots of firepower.

When Mario Sr. finally returned to action, he played two games and scored five points, then had to sit out with a pulled groin. He hated sitting out, but his recent agonies with his back had made him prudent: he wanted to be sure that he didn't do anything to reinjure his back. Mario returned to the lineup 50 games into the 1990–91 season. The Penguins had been a good team without him, with a 26-21-3 record. It was a good sign, for now Mario didn't have to carry the whole team on his fragile back. He could just play hockey.

With Mario making magic in his famous number 66 jersey, deking defenseman and fooling goalies and gen-erally making the puck look like it was Velcroed onto his stick, the Penguins maintained their pace, posting a 15-12-3 record. It was good enough to give them 88 points, and a first-place finish in their division. They won the Patrick (which was named in honor of their general man-ager's grandfather) for the first time in franchise history.

The Pens and Mario were confidant, and looking for-ward to doing something great in the playoffs. They may have been looking too far ahead because the first round, against the fourth-place finishers from their division, the New Jersey Devils, gave them a terrible scare. The Devils had the Pens down three games to two, and were looking to put the series away at home. Thanks to a Ron Francis goal, the Penguins kept the series alive, but then disaster struck in Game 7: Mario couldn't play. His back was bothering him.

Mario's doctors had told him to expect "back spasms," a painful condition that goes away with rest. So Mario had to sit in the stands as he watched his teammates defeat the Devils 4-2, and move to the next round against the Washington Capitals. The Caps, who had finished in third place behind Pittsburgh, gave the Pens another scare by winning the first game, but the Penguins came back and swept the next four games. They were now one series away from the Stanley Cup Final. And in between it and them were the Boston Bruins, who had finished first in their own division with 100 points.

The physical, gritty Bruins took a two-game lead at home, where their smaller ice surface made it hard for Pittsburgh's forwards to get open. Coach Johnson told Mario to hang back when the Pens were rushing, then come in late, in the hope that he could pick up the puck and burst through. Mario managed two goals and two assists in those first two games, but the Pens knew that they had to buckle down defensively when they went home to the Igloo.

With Mario taking charge and racking up 15 points in the series, the Penguins attacked and defended as if their lives depended on it, and won the next four games. Mario had made sure of it in Game 6, when he scored the empty net goal that put the Bruins into hibernation for the season. When the puck went in the net, Mario dropped to the ice on his knees, as if he was staggered by the weight of what they had done. Winning the next round meant winning the trophy that every hockey player dreams of winning: the Stanley Cup.

Their opponents would be the Minnesota North Stars, who had finished in fourth place in their division with 20 points less than Pittsburgh, but had become a Cinderella story with a surprise playoff run to the Stanley Cup Finals. The Penguins were hot and hungry, and Mario knew that all eyes would be on him to prove that he had the "right stuff." Wayne Gretzky had already shown that he had the "right stuff" *four times*.

The Penguins had lost the first game of each series so far, and this time they lost again. Though Mario scored a goal, he was on the ice when the North Stars scored three, and the Stars won 5-4. Mario later said that his legs wouldn't move as fast as he wanted them to, and that he had no energy. Everyone was thinking the same thing. Would his back hold up? Would it be the Memorial Cup bust all over again?

In the next game, Mario answered their worries with a magnificent performance scoring one of the greatest goals in Cup history. Minnesota had cut a 2-0 Pittsburgh lead in half and was coming on hard when Mario took an outlet pass from Phil Bourque. He charged up the ice toward Minnesota defenseman Shawn Chambers. Lemieux faked Chambers outside, then cut inside, and using his backhand, slid the puck between Chambers' legs.

He then raced by the flailing Minnesota d-man, picked up the puck on his forehand, and zeroed in on goalie Jon Casey, who was going to let Mario make the first move. Taking the puck from forehand to backhand, Mario lost his balance and slid to his knees. With Casey faked out of position, he slid the puck into an empty net. It was an amazing goal, with so many fakes that you had to watch it on slow motion replay to see the full beauty of it. And when you did, it was even more astonishing because Mario Lemieux had made the play at top speed.

The goal seemed to crush the will of the North Stars, and they lost the game, 4-1. However, the Minnesotans got a break when Mario's back problems flared up in Game 3. The pain was so bad that he couldn't bend over to tie up his skates. He had to sit out, and the Stars took advantage, winning 3-1 to take a one game lead.

Mario came back in Game 4 and scored a goal, helping his team to a 5-3 win. In the next game, he scored a goal and set up two more to give Pittsburgh the lead in the series for the first time. All they had to do was win one more game and the Cup was theirs. Would Mario rise to the occasion?

With the Pens leading 1-0, they took two penalties and had to defend against a 5-on-3 advantage for the North Stars. Mario chose this tough spot to shine. First he forced Minnesota's Mike Modano to take a penalty against him. Now the Penguins were only down one man. Next Lemieux stole the puck at the blue line and broke away from his pursuers to notch a short-handed goal. The

North Stars sagged as if they had lost already, which indeed they had, with the final score an embarrassing 8-0 for Pittsburgh. "It seemed like anything that was within 20 feet he reached," said Minnesota's Dave Gagner of Mario. "When somebody that big and that good wants to win that badly, there isn't much you can do."

And on that championship night, the Penguins, a bird that has never been known to take flight, soared. They had won it all. The critics couldn't say much about Mario now. Yes, he had missed more than 50 games, but he had five goals and seven assists in the championship series, and had won the Conn Smythe Trophy as the MVP in the playoffs. He had become the most dominant player in the game, and now he had the Stanley Cup. "You dream of this, but it's even better in real life than in your dreams," he said. But it wasn't just for him. That summer, he took Lord Stanley's trophy back to his parents' house on rue Jogues, where he had learned to skate on the living-room carpet. He sat in the kitchen with the Cup as the neighbors all came in to touch it, and to get autographs from the man whom they had long known was the best player in the world.

CHAPTER ELEVEN

Repeat

It is said that once you've won the Stanley Cup, you have to prove to people that you truly deserved it by winning it again. It's what the Penguins heard when they began their 1991–92 campaign, hoping to repeat as NHL champions. Pittsburgh winger Kevin Stevens, who had now proved himself to be a star, put it best. "When you win once, people wonder. When you win twice, it's no fluke."

Mario had spent the summer recovering from his extraordinary year. Despite the chance to play in another Canada Cup alongside Wayne Gretzky, he said no. This time, however, his reasons were clear to everyone. He did not want to strain his back by starting the season early. Instead, he would stay at home and play golf, basking in the sun, staying healthy for the next season. His own health was now foremost in his mind: he was going to be 27 in the autumn, and if he could stay injury-free, he hoped to have a few more Stanley Cup years under his belt by the time he retired. Yet when it came time to go to training camp, Mario was very worried about health. And it wasn't his own.

During the summer, his coach, "Badger" Bob Johnson, had taken Team USA on a tune-up tour in Western Canada in preparation for the Canada Cup. Johnson had always had problems with his teeth, so when he had a pain in his head on a flight back to Pittsburgh from Saskatchewan, he booked a visit to his dentist. His dentist could find nothing wrong with him, but just to be safe, sent him for a checkup. Before he could get to the doctor's, Johnson collapsed from what looked like a stroke. But it wasn't. He had cancer in his brain, and he didn't have long to live.

"I saw him about a week ago," Mario said, when he heard that the coach whom he liked so much was dying. "He was the same old Badger that everybody knows. It's really sad." Johnson's health declined quickly, and on November 26, 1991, he died. It was a devastating loss to the Penguins organization to whom Johnson had meant so much. It was especially devastating to Mario who had such a close relationship to the coach. The Penguins dedicated their season to him, and now, they were determined to make good on their promise to win another Stanley Cup.

There were other problems, though. The Penguins and three of their star players, Kevin Stevens, Ron Francis, and Mark Recchi, could not agree on contracts. It upset Mario who insisted that unless the team signed the trio, things looked grim. "I guess we're going to find out if the Penguins want to win another Stanley Cup," he said.

The Penguins eventually signed the three players, but there was trouble in management. The owner who had brought Mario into the NHL, Edward De Bartolo, was having financial problems and was forced to sell the team to a partnership of businessmen, Howard Baldwin, Morris Belzberg, and Thomas Ruta. The players were relieved that the team was going to stay in Pittsburgh, but were disconcerted that the season had started with so much difficulty.

With friendly, easygoing Bob Johnson gone, the Penguins had appointed Scotty Bowman as replacement coach. Bowman could be tough on his players, especially at practice. Eventually, the players were so annoyed with him that they asked for an assistant coach to run their practices in order to avoid conflict with Bowman.

The biggest problem of all, though, was Mario's back. He had had physiotherapy and surgery, and he had tried to rest his back in the off-season, but it was no use. His back would hurt when he bent over to tie his skates, or when he leaned into a slapshot, or when he made a quick stop and turn. The best that he could hope for when he woke up in the morning was that the pain was low enough to let him play that night. He would miss 16 games that season due to back trouble. And 16 games was nearly a quarter of the season.

When he did play, if his back didn't hurt him too badly, then the style of play in the NHL often did. Mario had seen it all before, when he was just a kid, and other players would try anything they could to stop him. But after a game against the Washington Capitals in January of 1992, he was extremely frustrated by the clutching, grabbing, hooking, and tripping that Washington had used against him and his teammates. He was even more frustrated that they chose not to call many penalties. After the game, Mario spoke out, "It's a skating and passing game

— that's what the fans want to see. The advantage is to the marginal player now. That's the way this garage league is run."

Mario's bold statement earned him a $1000 fine from NHL President John Ziegler. The President was angry that Mario had insulted the referees, the NHL, and the game. But many people, especially the skilled players who relied on their speed and their playmaking abilities to succeed, agreed with Mario. Later, Lemieux would meet with the President to discuss what he had said, and in the next few years, the league would agree with him too. Referees would become much more likely to call interference penalties.

To compound Mario's frustration, the Penguins traded his good friend Paul Coffey to L.A., and the talented Mark Recchi to Philadelphia for tough forward Rick Tocchet and big d-man Kjell Samuelsson. GM Patrick wanted to give the Penguins some grit for the playoffs — especially given the crash and bash kind of hockey that was being played that season.

Mario was sorry to see his friend Coffey go. They spent many hours off ice together, and Mario knew what kind of offensive threat Coffey could be on the ice, especially in the playoffs. But for ten days late in that season, it seemed as if there might not be any playoffs. The players went on strike, and everyone worried that there might not be a Stanley Cup series that season. Fortunately, the season was saved when players and management agreed to a settlement. Mario and the Penguins went off to defend their Cup title. They finished third in their division, with only two wins less than their Stanley Cup winning season, and in the first round of the playoffs, they would meet the Washington Capitals, the team which Mario had complained about earlier that year.

Things got off to a very bad start, with the Penguins going down three games to one. Mario knew that they were having defensive problems, so he spoke to coach Bowman, and then to the team after their 7-2 humiliation in Game 4. What the Penguins needed to do was send one man into the Washington zone after the puck, while the other four patrolled the neutral zone. This would stop the Capitals before they could get started. It worked, and Mario led the Penguins to an amazing comeback, with seven goals and ten assists. "We were beaten by one man," said Washington coach Terry Murray. "Number 66. Mario Lemieux. Right now, he's the best there is…"

The Penguins' victory meant that they had to face the New York Rangers, who had the best overall record that season in the NHL, and who hadn't won a Stanley Cup since 1940. The Rangers wanted the Cup badly. And they knew that one way or another, they had to stop Mario Lemieux if they were going to be the best.

In a cheap attempt to stop Mario in Game 2, New York forward Adam Graves used his stick like an axe, whacking Mario so hard on his left hand that he broke a bone in it. Graves was suspended for four games for his violent act; Mario, they said, would be out for three weeks.

Instead of feeling sorry for themselves, the Penguins rose to the occasion. With Tom Barrasso keeping pucks out of the net, and Ron Francis and Jaromir Jagr putting them in, they beat the Rangers in six games. Even better, Mario rejoined his team a week early, and led them to a four-game sweep of Boston. The Penguins would now take on the Chicago Blackhawks in the Stanley Cup Final.

Coaching the Hawks was Mike Keenan, the man who had coached Mario at his magnificent Canada Cup appearance in 1987. Keenan knew how good Mario could be, and so he tried to gain an advantage by attacking Mario in the press after he had scored the goal to give Pittsburgh a 5-4 win in Game 1 over Chicago, who had been leading 4-1 in the second period. Complaining about Mario's ability to draw penalties, Keenan decried, "I can't respect Mario for diving. The best player in the game is embarrassing himself and embarrassing the game."

Other coaches and players had accused Mario of diving before, of going down too easily to try to draw a penalty. Lemieux refused to be baited by Keenan, who was hoping to start a feud. "No comment," he said, when reporters asked him about Keenan's remarks. Then he smiled. "For now."

Once again, Mario preferred to do his talking on the ice. He scored the winning goal in Game 2, a 3-1 Pittsburgh win. He played defensively in Game 3, a 1-0 Pittsburgh win. In Game 4, the Penguins held on to a 6-5 lead to sweep the series, and once again call the Cup their own. The Penguins dominated the playoffs, leaving little doubt about how good they were. They had tied an NHL record by winning 11 consecutive games on their way to their second straight Cup. Mario's 34 points in the post-season — despite being sidelined for two weeks with a broken hand — was the best of any player in the playoffs. He won the Conn Smythe Trophy again as the most valuable player in the playoffs, and the Art Ross Trophy as the NHL's leading scorer with 44 goals and 87 assists. And he did it in a season where he had missed nearly a quarter of the Penguins' games. Once again he had come back from adversity to lead his team to victory. He was hoping now that he would get a year or two of good luck. Life, however, had other plans.

CHAPTER TWELVE

Captain Comeback

It had already been a bad year for Mario. He had been burdened with more back problems. He was facing potential legal and moral problems that came from being in the same hotel room where another player was accused of assaulting a woman (the player was never charged by the justice system). Then, in December 1992, Mario went to the doctor to complain of a lump on his neck and a sore throat. In January, the doctors told him the unthinkable: Mario Lemieux had Hodgkin's disease. Cancer.

If you have ever known anyone who has been told they have cancer, especially a friend or a family member, then you know how terrifying the word is. When you first hear it, cancer sounds like a death sentence, and too many times it is.

When Mario found out the news, he cried and cried before he could bring himself to tell his pregnant fiancée, Nathalie. What would he say to her? Not only was he in the prime of his hockey career, but he and Nathalie were in the prime of their lives. They were starting a family. This was no back injury. This disease could kill Mario. And what would happen to his family if he died?

When Mario told Nathalie, she cried too. Not for herself, but for him. How could this be happening to the man she believed was the greatest hockey player in the world? Hadn't he suffered enough?

When the hockey world found out about Mario's illness, many people cried, too. The shock was huge: Mario Lemieux had cancer. It was impossible. Mario's doctors tried to reassure both him and the hockey world that he had a good chance of beating this disease, but he knew in the back of his mind that when it came to cancer, no one could promise anything.

After all, two of his uncles had been killed by cancer, and a cousin of his had died from the same disease that he now had, one which affects the lymph nodes. The lymph nodes are found in the neck, armpits, above the groin, and near several large organs. They are part of the lymphatic system that helps the body to return fluids from its tissues to the circulatory system, and to fight infections. Hodgkin's disease, named after the English doctor who discovered it, progresses by enlarging the lymph nodes and inflaming major organs such as the liver. It usually affects men between the ages of 20-40, and if caught early, it can be successfully treated with radiation. Later cases are treated with drugs in a process called chemotherapy.

Mario knew all about chemotherapy and radiation. After all, he had already served as honorary chairman of the Pittsburgh Cancer Institute for the past five years. He had played in the charity golf tournaments and visited sick children. He had shaken hands with people who had lost their hair from chemotherapy, or their strength from radiation treatment. He had seen the look of desperate hope in their eyes.

Yet all was not as gloomy as it seemed. Mario had time on his side. His case had been diagnosed early, and the doctors decided to fight his cancer with radiation treatments. On January 13, the morning after Pittsburgh had announced Mario's illness, he walked into the locker room at the Igloo. He said hello to Kevin Stevens, Ron Francis, Rick Tocchet, and Ulf Samuelsson, but the room was tense. "As soon as I walked in, everything went silent," said Mario. "People aren't sure what to say. When somebody has cancer, there's not much you can say except, 'Good luck.'"

Two days later, Mario faced the media at a press conference. He put on a brave face. "I've faced a lot of battles since I was really young," he said, "and I've always come out on top. I expect that this will be the case with this disease." The press wanted to know when he would return to the ice. Mario's doctors said that he had a 95% chance of being cured, but a winner like Lemieux was aiming higher. "I'll be back when I'm 100% cured," he said. "Hopefully, that will be in time for the playoffs, and I can help us win another Stanley Cup, but first things first."

There was another worry as well. X-rays had shown shadows on Mario's lungs. The doctors at the press conference didn't mention that if those shadows were cancer as well, Mario's chances for survival were much worse. Even though the doctors thought Mario's cancer had not spread, he was scared. Once the cancer has begun to invade your body, the battle against it is a tough one.

Fortunately, Mario's doctors discovered that the shadows on his lungs had been caused by a case of mild pneumonia, so after two weeks on antibiotics to knock it out, Mario began his radiation treatments.

Every morning at 9 A.M., five days a week, Mario would drive to the medical center for his radiation treatment, which meant having his cancer bombarded with radioactive force. While radiation can destroy cancerous cells in your body, it also destroys healthy ones. And on top of this, your already sick body has to deal with the effects of having radioactive material pumped into it.

For four weeks, the hockey world held its breath as Mario went for his radiation treatments. In Pittsburgh, the phone-in radio sports shows had one topic: would Mario make it? In the streets, and restaurants, and bars, hockey fans talked about Lemieux as if he was everything the city stood for: loyalty, modesty, and an ability to win the big game. One sporting-goods storeowner spoke for the whole city when he said, "People in Pittsburgh just love this guy." The fans wanted to ensure that Mario knew how much they appreciated him and hoped it would give him strength.

So Mario took his radiation treatments and dug deep into his reserve of will, the will that made him take another shift when his back was so sore he couldn't even bend down to tie his own skates. He told himself that he would fight with everything he had. And he did.

One of the side effects of radiation is terrible fatigue, where walking up a flight of stairs can feel like playing triple overtime at full tilt. Since Mario was in such good shape from hockey, he fought off the fatigue so well that his doctors were astonished. Though he had lost a bit of weight, and had temporarily lost his sense of taste, Mario had held up amazingly well.

The doctors were even more astonished, and overjoyed, when after 22 radiation treatments, they were able to give Mario the best news possible: his cancer had gone into remission. It's what every cancer patient dreams of: the cancer had disappeared. "He's done extremely well, much better than I would have forecasted," said his doctor, James Hughes. "It's probably a function of his age, his physical fitness, and his desire." For the first time in a long time, Mario had something to celebrate. He was going to live.

And the news kept getting better. Though he would still need to be monitored for five years, Mario was cleared to play hockey again. Just a few short weeks ago, the hockey world had been contemplating the game without Lemieux, or worse, life without him. Yet after his last radiation treatment on March 2, 1993, one so hot it left a burn mark on his neck, Mario caught a plane to Philadelphia and pulled on his famous Number 66 that VERY night against the Flyers. The Philadelphia fans, who had no love for their state rival Penguins, gave Mario a 90-second standing ovation.

For a full minute and a half, the fans cheered Mario's return, and cancer's defeat, and life itself. Mario wasn't about to let down their enthusiasm, and so he responded in classic Mario fashion: he celebrated his return by scoring a goal and an assist. A few nights later, the Penguins played Los Angeles and Wayne Gretzky at home. Mario went head to head with his old rival and outdid him.

Mario scored a goal and an assist, and the Penguins won 4-3. This was no fluke, and people stopped holding their breath that Mario would somehow collapse and his return would be just an illusion. Mario was back. But that wasn't good enough. He wanted to be the best again.

Even though the Penguins finished first in their division, they lost the Division Final in the playoffs. Still, they had more to cheer about than they could have hoped for a few months earlier. Despite missing a large portion of the season, Mario Lemieux still won his fourth Art Ross Trophy as the NHL's top scorer, with 69 goals and 91 assists. But he had won so much more than that: he had not only defeated rival teams, he had defeated death. He was a symbol of life, a symbol of triumph over the coldest, deadliest disease. And people who had once felt him distant and remote now loved him for it.

CHAPTER THIRTEEN

Amazing!

Mario celebrated his victory over cancer by marrying his long-time girlfriend Nathalie Asselin in the summer of 1993. He was seeing life in vibrant color after his brush with death, and he knew more than ever that you had to separate what was important in life from what was not. Family was number one, and everything else came afterward. He was a father himself now, to a daughter, Lauren. He was 28 years old, and if everything went well, he had a few good years left to show the hockey world his magic.

As had always been the case with Mario, nothing was easy. The next season, his back troubles allowed him to play just 28 games, including six in the playoffs, when the Penguins were eliminated by the Washington Capitals. The following season, 1994–95, he didn't play at all. He stayed away from pro hockey for 17 months, hoping once and for all to heal his back, and recover from the effects of his cancer therapy in 1993. People wondered if they would ever see Mario in a Penguins' uniform again. They feared that his great career — some said greatest ever career — was going to be ended by injury and disease.

Mario wondered too, but he knew that if he wasn't going to play in the NHL ever again, it would not be through lack of effort. He had never liked working out with weights, or doing aerobic exercises like running and bike riding. He had felt that playing hockey every day was enough exercise, but now he thought differently. He no longer smoked. He had beaten cancer. And if he was going to come back to the NHL, then he was going to come back in style.

Two months before he took to the ice, Mario started to work out like he had never done before. "I lifted weights, worked on the bike, the treadmill," he said. "I actually put a gym in my home."

When Mario returned to the Penguins' training camp in 1995, everyone was delighted." It's great, it's unbelievable, it's like [Michael] Jordan coming back to basketball and people wanting to watch it," said Mario's former teammate Bob Errey. "We want to see if he can come all the way back. I know I do."

Mario returned to the NHL on September 20, 1995 in an exhibition game that the Penguins lost to Detroit. But no one was thinking anything about losing, they were thinking about what had been gained. Mario Lemieux was back yet again, and he looked great in the 20 minutes that he played, even if he was modest about his return.

"I made a lot of bad decisions, offensively and defensively," he said with a smile. "It's just a matter of getting back into the game. I haven't played hockey in such a long time, so it was a good test for me. I know I have a long way to go, but I feel good."

And so he did. Though the Penguins would not repeat as the Stanley Cup champions over the next two seasons, Mario lit up the league once again. He was so good that he won the Art Ross Trophy as the NHL's top scorer both in his latest "comeback" season and in the one after that. His sixth Art Ross Trophy would be his last. In 1997, Mario Lemieux announced that at the age of 31, he was hanging up his skates. He would be watching hockey from the stands, like everyone else.

During his final game in Pittsburgh on April 23, 1997, the 17,355 fans at the Civic Arena were bursting with emotion. Sure, the Penguins were down three games to nothing against the Philadelphia Flyers in the opening round of the Stanley Cup playoffs, but that wasn't the reason. The reason was Mario.

For the last five minutes of the game, the fans stood and cheered Mario. With just over a minute left, Mario took a breakout pass and found himself on a breakaway. He had been in this place so many times before, and with the roar of the crowd in his ears, he did what came so naturally to him. He scored a goal. It was as if Hollywood had written the moment — Mario scoring on his last shift, to help the Penguins to a 4-1 victory and keep their playoff hopes alive. The arena exploded with emotion, and Mario was no exception. "That was the first time I cried on the ice for a long time," he said later.

When he was named the game's first star, he took a victory lap on the ice and blew a kiss to the adoring fans. "I was just expressing my feelings to the crowd and how I feel about them," he said. It was a moment filled with love, and no small amount of sadness. People knew that they would never see another player like Lemieux again.

The Hockey Hall of Fame knew it as well, and waived the usual waiting period after a player retires. The rules didn't apply to someone like Lemieux. "I just want to be remembered as somebody who was able to take a team that was the worst in the league and was able to bring a championship to Pittsburgh. I'm very proud that I accomplished that. And, hopefully, I'll be remembered as a winner."

Mario had no idea what was to lie ahead. He expected to be spending much more time with his wife and four children, when he wasn't playing his beloved golf. Yet once again, life placed an obstacle in his way just when he thought he had made it through safely. This time it wasn't his health that was threatened, it was his financial security.

In 1992, Mario had signed a $42 million US contract with Pittsburgh owner Howard Baldwin. In 1997, another owner named Roger Marino bought into the team. Under Mario's contract, he was to be paid in full if anyone other than Howard Baldwin took over the team. Roger Marino was making more of the team's day-to-day decisions, and he refused to pay Mario the $33 million that was owed. Mario wasn't the only one who was owed money: the Penguins owed $110 million US. The team had sought protection from their creditors under US bankruptcy laws after losing millions.

Mario knew that unless he did something, he was going to lose the financial rewards he so deserved after such a stellar but trying career. So he went to court to try to get paid. When that didn't work, he did something that no NHL hockey player — in fact, no professional athlete — had ever done: he became an owner of the team. Because the Penguins could not pay him the money he was owed, Mario joined a group of investors to buy the team that he had made into a champion.

It was amazing. Mario had won six scoring titles and two Stanley Cups. He had endured painful back problems, surgery, and infection. He had beaten cancer and made the Hall of Fame. And now, at only 33, he owned his own hockey team. And suddenly, the chance for the Penguins to get out of the mess that they were in looked a lot better.

With Mario involved, the city of Pittsburgh did everything they could to help the new ownership group to save the Penguins. They forgave debts and reduced rents. Mario said he would try to sell more season tickets and then sign the four or five players who would take the Penguins to the level they wanted to be: winners of another Stanley Cup.

It was Jaromir Jagr who summed up the feelings for everyone. "When I heard the news I was so happy, happy for Mario and happy for the city," said Mario Jr. "Mario saved hockey in Pittsburgh 15 years ago, and now he's doing it again." What Jagr couldn't have imagined was that Mario was going to be a very unusual owner — one who would be the best player on the team.

Epilogue

When Mario Lemieux stepped back into the NHL on December 27, 2000, he had been away from pro hockey for 44 months. He was now 35 years old and a father of four, and his main form of exercise was playing golf. When Mario announced that he was planning to make another comeback, perhaps his biggest yet, there was joy in hockeyland. Mario coming back was like a dream come true not only for his four-year-old son Austin, who simply wanted to see his father play for the first time, but for all hockey fans.

A capacity crowd had squeezed into Pittsburgh's Mellon Arena to witness the magician's return, along with a horde of international media. The CBC television play-by-play man kept comparing the night to a movie, while one of the Penguins managers compared Mario to Batman. "He's a suit-wearing executive by day. At night he puts on his cape and plays." Everyone was excited in a way they hadn't been since they were kids at Christmas, and now, two days after Christmas, they were getting a huge present. And the spotlight of the hockey world was on Mario, ready to follow every glorious move he made.

It didn't take him long. Just 33 seconds into the game against the Toronto Maple Leafs, Mario set up a goal. Later that night he set up another, and for good measure, he also scored on a pass from Jagr. The arena went crazy with standing ovations, and the Penguins won the game 5-0. A couple of nights later in the second game of his return, Mario scored an empty net goal and three assists as the Penguins beat Ottawa 5-3. Mario was not only back, he was as good as ever.

So good, in fact, that when the regular season ended, Mario had 35 goals and 41 assists in just 43 games. Sure, Mario didn't finish at the top of the scoring chart. Mario's teammate Jaromir Jagr did that, winning the scoring title with 52 goals and 69 assists. Jagr registered 121 points in 81 games, which gave him an average of one and a half points per game. Astonishingly, the math suggests even better statistics for Mario. Then you'll see the nature of his accomplishment. In 43 games he tallied 76 points, which gives an average of nearly two points per game (1.77 to be exact). Or better than the guy who was the best scorer in the league, and who played 36 more games than Lemieux.

It was even more amazing because Mario returned to NHL for the toughest part of the season, the second half, when teams and players are gunning to get in the Stanley Cup. The fact that he did so well after watching from the stands for the previous three and a half years is further evidence that those who call him "the best" are not exaggerating.

When the Stanley Cup playoffs rolled around, hockey fans everywhere were talking about Mario Lemieux. Not only had he made an amazing comeback, but he had led his team into a playoff position. The Penguins finished with 96 points, putting them third in the Atlantic division. In the first round, the Penguins met the Washington Capitals. The series was tight, but Mario and the Penguins pulled it off, winning 4 games to 2.

People who still doubted Mario said that beating Washington proved nothing. If Mario was to make this season into the beginning of an impossible dream, then the Penguins would have to beat their next opponents, the Buffalo Sabres.

The Sabres had finished second in the Northeast division, with 98 points. Even though that was only two points better than the Penguins, some hockey analysts said that the Sabres were strong contenders to win the Stanley Cup. They had a potent chemistry, one that combined offensive talent with defensive grit, and that "something extra" that is hard to define, but that championship teams always have it. And as if that wasn't enough, they also had Vezina Trophy winning Dominik "The Dominator" Hasek in net.

All the Penguins had in goal was a young Swede named Johan Hedberg, who had only 9 games of NHL experience before he found himself playing for Lord Stanley's trophy. And oh yes, the Penguins had Jaromir Jagr and Mario Lemieux.

Young Hedberg shut out Buffalo in the first game, and only allowed one goal in the second, but the Sabres came roaring back to win three games straight, the last of those in overtime. Now they could put the Penguins — and the story of Mario's incredible comeback — away for good. The Sabres knew Mario liked to golf, and they wanted to give him an early start on the golf course. But there was one thing standing in their way: Mario.

Things didn't look good for the Penguins in their do-or-die game. With under two minutes to play in regulation time in Game 6, Pittsburgh was on the wrong end of a 2-1 score. As the clock ticked down, indifferent to the Penguins' desperation, the players on the ice and on the bench all knew that it was soon going to be over unless something big happened. Then suddenly, Mario's magic came alive in the way that it had so many times before.

With just 78 seconds left on the clock, there was a scramble in front of the Buffalo net. The puck popped into the air, and no one could find it. Players flailed about trying to see where the little black disk had gone, but only one player knew exactly where it was. Mario Lemieux caught the puck in flight with his eye, and when it bounced on the ice right at his feet, he banged it home. The games was tied. The Penguins were alive.

The Penguins' bench erupted in cheers as if they had just won the Stanley Cup. Mario had saved their season. One All-Star goalie who was watching the game just shook his head. He could only explain Mario's magic as the force of a higher power. "It's like Mario sometimes has divine intervention at his fingertips," said New Jersey Devils goalie Martin Brodeur. "I saw the game on TV, and I still don't believe it. The puck has a way of finding him, no matter where he is."

Inspired by their leader's heroics, the Penguins went on to win the game in overtime, then finish off the Sabres in another overtime battle in Game 7. People were now talking about the most incredible comeback in the history of hockey, or of any sport.

Their next opponents were the defending Stanley Cup Champions, the New Jersey Devils. After losing the first game to the Devils, the Penguins bounced back in the second. Once again, Mario sparked his team, who were down 2-0 when a Mario rebound led to a short-handed Pittsburgh goal. Less than three minutes later, Mario hopped over the boards, stole the puck from Devils defenseman Ken Daneyko, and in one smooth motion, put it on the stick of Alexei Kovalev, who tied the score. The Penguins added two more goals, and their 4-2 victory evened the series at a game apiece. "When we scored, everybody started believing," said goalie Johan Hedberg. "Once again Mario was there for us at a crucial time."

But then, just when the Penguins were beginning to see themselves in the glinting silver of the Stanley Cup, the magic stopped. Suddenly the Penguins couldn't score, the Devils set John Madden and Scott Stevens loose on Mario to shut him down. They were all over him, hooking, jabbing, smothering, slashing, and generally making life miserable. Mario was frustrated, and he took some bad penalties. The other Penguins couldn't pick up the slack, and the team played as if they were skating in slush. When the Devils won the series 4 games to 1, Mario's dream of a Stanley Cup fairytale ending was over, at least for the year. And so, it seemed, was his long partnership with the gifted but moody Jaromir Jagr. All through the playoffs, Jagr had made noises about how he would not be a Pittsburgh Penguin come training camp in September. Now that the Penguins' season was over, Mario put on his team owner's hat and all but gave Jagr his wish. "He's still the best player in the world," said Mario. "We hope to keep all our players, but life goes on."

Indeed it does, though when Mario looked back on his 2001 playoff run, he could take pride in what he had done. With 6 goals and 11 assists, he led the Penguins in points. He finished in eighth place in the playoff scoring race, but with three game-winning goals, he was tied for first place in that category with, among others, the league's MVP and Stanley Cup champ, Joe Sakic of Colorado.

As a testament to how spectacular a comeback Mario had made, and perhaps in part a celebration of his glorious return to hockey, Mario was named captain of Canada's Olympic hockey team for the Winter 2002 Olympic Games by none other than Wayne Gretzky, now the Olympic team boss. Mario will lead his country into the hunt for Olympic Gold. And why not? He is golden himself. He has shown beyond a doubt that he is truly the best.

One of the NHL's most thoughtful players, Igor Larionov, tried to understand Mario's remarkable come-back and found his world of comparison not in sport, but in art. "Mario is the bright color of the game," he said. "People want to see a Monet, a Rembrandt at work. Whenever he's on the ice, he's capable of producing a masterpiece, or at least the unpredictable or unexpected. It's art, hockey performed at its highest skill level. If people are appreciating him more now, it's like an artist who gains proper recognition only after he passes away. But he lives again."